WE
WERE
THERE,
TOO

WE WERE THERE, TOO

PIONEERING APPALACHIAN TRAIL WOMEN

Gwenyth L. Loose

APPALACHIAN TRAIL
CONSERVANCY®

Harpers Ferry

First edition

Published by the Appalachian Trail Conservancy
    799 Washington Street (P.O. Box 807)
    Harpers Ferry, West Virginia 25425-0807
    <www.appalachiantrail.org>

ISBN 978-1-944958-11-4

Library of Congress Control Number: 2020944380

TABLE OF CONTENTS

INTRODUCTION

My introduction to the Appalachian Trail was so ordinary that I cannot explain why, after nearly fifty-five years, I so vividly recall the experience. It was one of those rare, late-November days — Thanksgiving Day to be exact — when Mother Nature provided the bluest of skies and a mild temperature.

Dad was given his orders, delivered sternly by my mother, "Get these kids outside. For Pete's sake [her favorite expletive], this dinner will never get on the table with them tromping through the kitchen!"

And so, my brother and I, along with our beagle, Queenie, were ushered to the rear seat of our family's pale-yellow Rambler station wagon. Our uncle hustled into the front seat, and Dad drove off with only the briefest of explanation that we were going hiking on a trail. No destination was mentioned. No provisions were taken except for Queenie's leash, for she was a great hunter, prone to take off with the slightest smell of game — rabbit, squirrel, or deer.

We traveled a familiar road, the Wertzville Road, along the edge of the great Cumberland Valley near our central Pennsylvania home and parked in a small, gravel lot.

Our adventure was brief. We walked up a dirt road to the top of the mountain, then along the ridge for approximately thirty minutes before doing an about-face and returning to the car. Nothing remarkable at all in this brief adventure, except that blue sky, unseasonably warm sun, and a noticeable energy in our dad's footsteps as he explained to us that we were walking on the

Appalachian Trail. He cautioned us that if we didn't turn around, we would end up in Georgia and far, far away from our turkey dinner.

I distinctly remember my brother and I standing in the middle of that forested path and gazing down the trail with wide-eyed wonder, then turning to catch up to our dad and uncle. Our immediate attention shifted to home and Thanksgiving dinner, as we turned our backs, for now, on a hiking adventure of a length that we could hardly begin to imagine.

Quite naturally, my first acknowledgment is to my father. He loved the outdoors, although I would not characterize him as a great outdoorsman. Sure, he dabbled in fishing, hunting, gardening — those types of outdoor activities — but we were a working-class family, and his time was most often consumed with earning a modest living as a car inspector for the Pennsylvania Railroad. But, from him, I grew to love the outdoors. Mine was a childhood filled with building forts, making mud pies, and stomping around our neighborhood in my treasured cowgirl outfit. When the time came to leave for college, my mother spent hours making the tiniest of stitches to sew name tags on every article of clothing that I was to pack, while I headed to the local shoe store to buy a pair of boy's work boots. Those became my first hiking boots, as I filled my weekends with visiting nearby state parks.

Hiking became a favorite pastime that would endure and grow throughout my adult years. I've officially traded my childhood mudpie recipes for some of the best, high-energy, trail-cookie recipes, and the cowgirl outfit has been replaced with my favorite zip-off hiking pants and wick-away shirt. Yes, I grew up, and my passion for hiking and all things outdoors also grew. Thanks, Dad!

I returned to the Appalachian Trail while pursuing a master's degree in American studies at Pennsylvania State University. Another fall hike along the Trail — this time with fellow graduate student Debra Smith — ended with a brief conversation on the lack of information about the women who worked to build, protect, and preserve the Appalachian Trail. Although we were both reading extensively about the early history of the Trail project, as we walked along this canopied trail, neither of us could name one woman featured in any of the Trail literature. This conversation planted the seed for an independent study during which I began research at the archives of the Appalachian Trail Conservancy and Potomac Appalachian Trail Club, focused not so much on female Appalachian Trail hikers, but rather on the women who assumed leadership roles in the Trail project. Who were they and what were their contributions?

Here I discovered three women whose work spanned from the early 1930s when the Trail project was in its infancy through the 1990s as the popularity of the Trail was exploding. And so, my second acknowledgment is to Debra Smith and my professors at Pennsylvania State University who inspired me to pursue an intellectual adventure that led to the writing of this book. Thank you for instilling in me the urge to dig into Appalachian Trail archives, a determination to uncover the histories of these Appalachian Trail women, and an appreciation for the scholarly processes required to accurately portray each woman.

Years have passed since completing my graduate studies, with time filled with my favorite activities of hiking, reading, and researching — all focused almost exclusively on the Appalachian Trail. Then I met Larry Luxenberg, founder of the Appalachian Trail Museum. Before long, Larry molded me into the museum exhibit curator and began prodding me to expand my thesis into a full-fledged book on A.T. women. And so, my third recognition is to Larry Luxenberg, a master of Trail history in his own right, who knew when to listen and when to push.

The evolution of this book was slow, hampered by my eight-to-five commitment (also called "a job"), volunteer museum work, and, of course, answering the call of the Trail on weekends to hike. Others who faithfully pushed me onward, and to which I owe a mountain of gratitude, include ATC publisher Brian King, who knows a good story and has mastered how to tell it; reader-editor Margy Schmidt with her exceptional ability to know right from wrong within the entire English language; my daughters, Sarah and Emily, who inspire me to reach high, and my many friends in the York

Hiking Club whose regular inquiries about my progress toward completing this book served to instill in me a bit of embarrassment. And so, I wrote this book that you now hold in your hands. May it bring you hours of learning, moments of wonder, and an itch in your feet to walk the Appalachian Trail.

In choosing Jean Stephenson, Ruth Blackburn, and Margaret Drummond as my subjects, I was able to present to the reader three previously untold stories of women whose contributions spanned three distinct eras of Appalachian Trail history. Jean was there almost from the beginning, and, as such, her greatest contributions were toward the initial building of the Trail and the garnering of early support. Ruth was in the forefront of the struggles to secure the corridor during the critical years when development threatened the very existence of the Appalachian Trail. Margaret safeguarded the role of volunteers and maintaining clubs as the Appalachian Trail Conference morphed into the Appalachian Trail Conservancy with increased focuses on strategic planning, operational efficiencies, and responding to many 21st-century issues.

Ensuring the future of the Appalachian Trail was a goal common to these women, but their experiences were starkly different. Whereas Jean Stephenson spent the early years arguing with editors of national magazines to print articles about a little-known and still-not-completed Appalachian ridgeline trail, Ruth Blackburn and Margaret Drummond were each deeply engaged in a mature maintaining-club system — Ruth in the Potomac Appalachian Trail Club and Margaret in the Georgia Appalachian Trail Club.

While studying these three women offers a rare window into three distinct chapters in the history of the Appalachian Trail, many other women have made notable contributions to its building, maintenance, and protection. In highlighting Jean, Ruth and Margaret, we celebrate them all. As the Appalachian Trail evolved from a little-known footpath into a national scenic trail visited by hikers from around the world, the stories of women of the Appalachian Trail acclaim, "We were there, too!"

— *Gwenyth Loose*

CHAPTER 1

IN THE BEGINNING

Underneath an absurdly large, flouncy hat, her eyelids fluttered and finally closed as Henriette d'Angeville nestled further into the white snows of France's Mont Blanc. Layers of heavy skirts and a fur cloak — most unsuitable for mountain climbing — wrapped around Henriette as she curled herself comfortably into the mountain's formidable slope. All too aware of the dangers of allowing sleep to overcome climbers at elevations above fifteen thousand feet, her male guides watched Henriette appear evermore oblivious to the frighteningly cold and thin air. None of them had ever taken a lady up Mont Blanc, and, despite her present state, they knew Henriette to be courageous and determined. But, how to wake her? How to make her aware of the dangers they all faced if she did not regain her feet and move forward toward the summit?

"We must wake her!" one guide exclaimed.

"Perhaps she is already dead," another offered.

"Impossible!" Joseph-Marie Couttet, the head guide, grumbled.

Henriette groaned, sat up, shook her head with indifference to her situation and then toppled back into her snow bed. Couttet swore under his breath. One of the younger guides boldly stepped forward, and, with the intent to appeal to Henriette's pride and extreme aversion to any form of failure, he bent down close to her face, questioning, "Should I carry her? I can do it. I'm still strong enough."

His offer penetrated Henriette's consciousness. She rose to her knees, grabbed her hiking stick, and hosted herself up on unsteady feet. "I will not be carried!" she exclaimed as the glint returned to her eyes. She turned to face the snowy slope. "I intend to make the whole journey on my own two feet.

Truly there would not be much merit in going up Mont Blanc on someone else's back!"

To the male guides who accompanied Henriette d'Angeville as she stubbornly reached the summit of Mont Blanc in 1838, her achievement marked a turning point in mountaineering history. Henriette's accomplishment helped to break through the age-long belief that the "fairer sex" could not endure the strenuous activity of mountain climbing nor could their "weaker constitutions" survive in harsh climates and thin, oxygen-depleted environments. Although Henriette's achievement on Mont Blanc is today little-known, societal perceptions of what women could achieve in the outdoors began to crumble in the nineteenth century.

Henriette d'Angeville

True to the pioneer spirit that settled North America, women set out with a determination to experience mountain adventures on this continent. History reveals that they were not following in Henriette's footsteps but rather preceding her Mont Blanc accomplishment by nearly seventeen years. Particularly in the northeastern region of the United States, several accomplishments by women in many ways rival that of Henriette's and helped to set the stage for female participation in projects such as the Appalachian Trail and in hiking organizations such as the Appalachian Trail Conference and its maintaining clubs. From the Austin sisters' summit of New Hampshire's Mount Washington in 1821 to the ascent of Maine's remote Katahdin by Hannah Keep and Esther Jones in 1848, American women were raising "the glass ceiling" on this side of the Atlantic Ocean.

Just as the French hailed each successful assent of Mont Blanc, the earliest American adventurers to be considered mountaineers regarded New Hampshire's Mount Washington with awe and trepidation. (Darby Field took two Abenakis on two superstition-busting treks to the summit in 1642.) Since an ascent by an all-male group of scientists in 1784, Mount Washington has held tenaciously on to its reputation for changeable, severe weather. Manassed Cutler, who offered the most detailed account of the 1784 expedition, agreed with the calculation of Mount Washington's height as close to ten thousand feet — an over-estimation of nearly four thousand feet. And, at the time, he could list only four peaks in the world higher — Andes, Peak of Teneriffa, Gamoni, and the notorious Mont Blanc. Accordingly, when three young sisters, Eliza, Harriet, and Abigail Austin, visited the guest house of Ethan and Lucy Crawford in New Hampshire's White Mountains in August 1821, the Crawfords were not quite prepared to welcome this new breed of female adventurer.

After losing their first home in the notch between Mount Webster and Mount Willey in the Presidential Range to a fire in July 1818, Ethan moved a small house to their home site and, over several years, expanded their home to serve as an inn for settlers transporting goods between the upper Connecticut River Valley and the seaport towns of Portland, Maine, and Portsmouth, New Hampshire. Ethan and Lucy soon found their inn welcoming hundreds of horse-drawn sleighs each week when snow covered the ground, as tradesmen hauled pork, cheese, butter, and other farm products through the notch and on to New England markets. With the notion of further expanding his business by promoting the area's mountains as a place for outdoor adventure, Ethan and his father, Abel, cut a primitive trail to the summit of nearby Mount Washington.

In the spring of 1821, Ethan, assisted by a young surveyor, blazed a much-improved path to Mount Washington's summit. Soon afterward, the Crawford inn began welcoming more and more refined city-dwellers who were seeking adventures in the White Mountains under the relative comfort and safety of local guides such as Ethan and other Crawford men. Although early groups all consisted of male adventurers, Ethan's notoriety as "the mountain giant" capable of conquering the area's peaks and Lucy's fame for making her guests comfortable and well-fed soon attracted tourists of the "fairer sex," such as the Austin sisters.

Each newly cut trail improved access to the once-remote summits within the White Mountains, quite naturally inviting adventuresome women to do more than gaze upon these lofty heights from the comfort of the Crawford inn. No longer feeling the traditional restrictions to watch as husbands, brothers, sons, and fathers set out at dawn for mountain adventures nor to listen as they returned home at dusk boasting of their mountaineering prowess, women guests began requesting that the Crawfords guide them to the nearby summits.

On August 31, 1821, when Eliza, Harriet, and Abigail Austin arrived at the Crawfords' Old Moosehorn Tavern with the intent to become the first women to walk to the summit of Mount Washington, Ethan just recently had completed his second path to its summit. However, suffering from a recent ax wound to his heel, he was not prepared to serve as guide. Instead, two local men served as guides — Charles Stuart, a veteran of one year's climbing experience, who was engaged to Eliza, and a tenant of the Austin farm who was to carry the ladies' baggage. Their brother, Daniel Austin, would also accompany them.

The Austin sisters were not experienced hikers, nor were they inclined to abandon their long skirts, which caught on the rocks and roots of the newly cut, seven-mile approach trail and became heavy with rain as they spent two of their three nights at the same primitive camp while waiting out a storm. Despite those days of floundering on the approach trail and requiring Ethan to eventually hobble on a cane to come to their assistance, Eliza, Harriet, and Abigail each reached Mount Washington's summit on the fourth day. To the young sisters, their adventure was a success. However, to Ethan — and many other men, to be sure — the Austin sisters' experience did not convince them that women were capable of true mountaineering. Nevertheless, over time, Ethan began to do what he could to make the climbing routes easier and safer. He built additional camps and improved the approach trails in order for hikers to face the final assents with greater reserves of energy. Finally, in 1825, his wife, Lucy, succeeded in accompanying Ethan to the summit of Mount Washington, and, by the late 1820s, women were no longer a rarity on many peaks across the White Mountains.

Eliza, Harriet, and Abigail Austin were most likely the first women in the United States to climb a significant mountain. Along with their French mountaineering counterpart, Henriette d'Angeville, the Austin sisters were pathbreakers both in physical accomplishments and social barriers. Yet, even as women began to trickle into America's mountainous regions and hiking communities, their acceptance was cautiously slow. A journal entry in the Crawford guesthouse registry states:

> *Gentlemen, there is nothing in the ascent of Mount Washington that you need dread. Ladies, give up all thought of it; but, if you are resolved, let the season be mild, consult Mr. Crawford as to the prospects of the weather, and with every precaution, you will still find it, for you, a tremendous undertaking.*

Despite such cautions, women continued to reach the summits of many of America's northeastern mountains. Mrs. Daniel Patch made the ascent of Moosilauke around 1840, enjoying a proper brew of tea on the summit from the teapot she carried to the top. A year earlier, in New York's Adirondack Mountains, a fifteen-year-old farm girl, Esther McComb, defied the prohibitions of her parents as she set out for the summit of Whiteface. She never made it to Whiteface but rather was rescued by a search party after climbing what later was named Mount Esther — still a noteworthy, mountaineering accomplishment by a young, inexperienced farm girl.

In August 1849, two groups of female climbers competed to become the first women to reach the summit of Maine's Katahdin. In retrospect, that particular objective has clear connection to the yet-to-be-conceived Appalachian Trail, since, as that project evolved nearly seventy-five years later, Katahdin would come to be identified as the northern terminus of this long-distance through-trail following the Appalachian Mountains.

When five women under the leadership of a "forceful and prickly" Marcus Keep set out for Katahdin's summit in the summer of 1849, local resentment was aroused. A second female party consisting of Mrs. E. Oakes Smith, an accomplished mountaineer, and two men took on the challenge of depriving Keep's group of the notoriety of taking the first women hikers to Katahdin's summit. A women's race to the summit ensued.

On August 11, Mrs. Smith and her fellow hikers reached what they declared to be the "Top of Mount Katahdin," as they stated quite arrogantly in a note left for the Keep party to discover a week later. Keep and his group of five women, upon finding the note, continued undisturbed across the Knife Edge, where he later wrote, "no foot of better halves had been," then proceeded to reach South Peak. From there, Hannah Taylor Keep and Esther Jones continued to the last summit of the ridge, which is today regarded as Katahdin's true summit. There, the two women piled rocks upon rocks to mark their accomplishment. It is quite possible that the cairn they built that day was the first constructed on that summit and serves as the forerunner of the iconic cairn that stands today at the northern terminus of the Appalachian Trail.

Justifiably, the footprint those two women left at the summit of Katahdin was more than a simple, feminine presence. Perhaps it was the genesis of an Appalachian Trail legacy that has endured to this day. In either case, on August 20, 1848, Hannah Keep and Esther Jones' ascent of Katahdin earned them a place in women's mountaineering history, and their simple actions of placing rock upon rock on Katahdin's summit arguably made a significant contribution to the role of women in Appalachian Trail history.

Barriers still existed for women determined to be a part of America's growing interest in the outdoor activities of hiking and mountain climbing and the expanding formation of trail clubs. But, the accomplishments of those women in New Hampshire's White Mountains, and others continents away, such as Henriette d'Angeville, were disproving all traditional perceptions of the "fairer sex's" mental and physical limitations. As Lucy Crawford would later write in her *History of the White Mountains*, regarding the Austin sisters, but also descriptive of these women pioneers of hiking:

> *I think this act of heroism ought to confer an honor on them, as everything was done with so much prudence and modesty by them: There was not left a trace or even a chance for a reproach or slander excepting by those who thought themselves outdone by these young ladies.*

Lucy and her contemporaries were not yet ready to throw off their long skirts in favor of more sensible hiking attire, such as bloomers or slacks, but the stage was set for women in greater numbers to take to the mountains — especially in the more progressive, urban areas surrounding the eastern Appalachian Mountain range. No longer content to sit on the Crawford Inn's porch and gaze upward at lofty mountain peaks, women were now determined to experience the sublime.

Conceiving the conception that a footway the length of the Appalachian Range would be something worth having.....

— *Benton MacKaye*

CHAPTER 2

THE EARLY YEARS

The project to create a trail along the Appalachian Mountain ridgeline still is seen as largely the product of two men, Benton MacKaye and Myron Avery. Often referred to as the Trail's "founding fathers," those two men brought their respective genius to the project. MacKaye, as a regional planner and "big thinker," first presented the idea; Avery provided the passionate drive needed to take an idea for a footpath and place it on the ground. They were very different men with very different views for this ridgeline footpath, but together they provided the leadership to create the Appalachian Trail. And, while women appear very early in the history of the Appalachian Trail, the story truly begins with those two talented men — MacKaye and Avery.

When Benton MacKaye's article, "An Appalachian Trail: A Project in Regional Planning," appeared in the *Journal of the American Institute of Architects* in October 1921, MacKaye knew that his work had only just begun. Often referred to as the visionary or "dreamer" of the Appalachian Trail, MacKaye, nevertheless, had a well-grounded sense of what would be required to turn his dream into a reality — he needed to recruit to his cause an influential group of supporters. Or, expressed in today's terms, MacKaye needed to network with key stakeholders.

A young Benton MacKaye (center) hiking with college friends Sturgis Pray (left) and J.W. Draper (Courtesy of Dartmouth College Library).

Envisioning large regional projects was not new to MacKaye. In fact, many may argue that his life was spent dreaming big, or, again using more contemporary language, MacKaye was a master of thinking outside the box. Born on March 6, 1879, in Stamford, Connecticut, to playwright and producer Steele MacKaye and the equally literary Mary Medbery, MacKaye was one of six children and the youngest son. The MacKaye household, being far from typical of New England families during America's Victorian Age, provided the young MacKaye with just the right mix of wealth and financial woes, structure and freedom, city and country living, formal education and outdoor roaming to spur his intellect.

In July 1887, at age eight, Benton, his mother, aunt, and siblings spent their first of many summers at a small cottage in Shirley Center, Massachusetts — the cottage being purchased with earnings from the early acting experiences of his older brother, Will. The Shirley cottage would become MacKaye's lifelong home. Regardless of wherever he may reside during various stages of his life, he always returned to this cottage. Family summers at Shirley Center offered the youthful MacKaye daily freedom to explore the countryside. Of course, those ramblings were not the ordinary, carefree frolics through forests and meadows taken by most young boys. Rather, MacKaye took a more academic approach to his outdoor adventures, dubbing them "Expeditions." Together with several cowanderers, he formed the Rambling Boys Club; MacKaye's "Geographical

The MacKaye family "cottage" in Shirley Center, from Benton's glass-slides collection.

Hand Book" documented their travels and observations. Even at this early age, Benton's actions were deliberate, his travels purposeful, and his journaling indicative of someone who considered his discoveries to be of great importance and his reflections to be provocative. While but a small boy, Benton was already beginning to have big thoughts.

At age eleven, Benton, accompanied by his mother, aunt, and youngest two siblings, spent the winter of 1890 in a Washington, D.C., rooming house as his father's theatrical career reached its lowest ebb. The two eldest brothers found employment in government offices, providing at least temporary financial stability for their transplanted household. MacKaye continued his explorations, this time within the great halls of the Smithsonian Institution and the adjoining United States National Museum rather than the Shirley Center countryside. There MacKaye befriended staff members, spent hours perched on a camp stool sketching specimens from the museum's extensive exhibits, attended lectures, and, in general, became immersed in the museum's natural history.

"Expedition 9" occurred in the summer of 1893, while Benton was fourteen and once again exploring the natural environment of the family's summer home at Shirley Center. One particular day's ramble is often identified as giving birth to MacKaye's thinking about a long, ridgeline footpath. In his journal entry of June 12, 1893, he reflects on the day's ramble to nearby Hunting Hill: "The hill itself is a drumling. As I sit looking off this drumling only 542 feet high, taking in the beauty of scenery, I have the country spread out like a map before me." Even in his early adolescence, MacKaye was envisioning broad landscapes and describing them using an unconventional vocabulary.

During a 1952 interview by Potomac Appalachian Trail Club (PATC) member Dorothy Martin, recounted in *A Footpath in the Wilderness: The Early Days of PATC*, MacKaye recalls another youthful expedition that marked a step toward his "conceiving…that a footway the length of the Appalachian Range would be something worth having." His companions were James Sturgis Pray and Draper Maury; the time was August 1897. Having weathered his freshman year at Harvard, MacKaye and his two college companions set out by bicycle from Shirley Center, headed for the hill towns of southern New Hampshire. From there, they tramped for several weeks throughout New Hampshire's White Mountains. MacKaye recalled in the 1952 interview that it was during this time that the notion evolved for creation of "a path through a pathless woods." Although appearing to be a paradox or even a contradiction, this concept matured into MacKaye's signature big idea for a primeval wilderness experience, a concept he defended throughout his long life as intrinsic to the Appalachian Trail. In effect, this notion of "a path through a pathless woods" became MacKaye's North Star — guiding his thinking about a primitive footpath along the Appalachian Mountains.

Following his graduation from Harvard in 1900, MacKaye continued his ramblings throughout New England while taking on various stints as a private tutor and camp counselor. In 1903, while continuing to grapple with establishing a clear career path, MacKaye would again accompany Sturgis Pray to the White Mountains as Pray began to lay out the first through-trail in that area. Pray was now councillor of improvements of the Appalachian Mountain Club, a position that inspired him to pioneer and defend the position of keeping improvements out of wilderness areas. This return visit to the White Mountains further galvanized MacKaye's notion of long-distance, primitive footpaths. Although MacKaye's concept of placing such a trail along the crest of the Appalachian chain was still nearly two decades into the future, his backwoods experiences with Sturgis Pray introduced MacKaye to the rigors and pleasures of tramping through pathless woods. Indeed, a bold notion was brewing.

There is something more at stake here than the preservation of the scenery.

— William T. Howell

Coincidentally, while MacKaye's regional thinking about the Appalachian wilderness continued to mature through his adult years, the Northeast was becoming a hotbed for the building of new trails and the linking of existing trails. The idea for an Appalachian through-trail was on the verge of discovery, both conceptually by MacKaye and on-the-ground by such New England trail builders as Professor Will S. Monroe in Vermont's Green Mountains; the trio of Charles Blood, Paul Jenks, and Nathaniel Goodrich in New Hampshire's White Mountains; and an army of trail-cutters under the direction of Major William A. Welch of New York's Harriman–Bear Mountain State Park, elements of the Palisades Interstate Park, of which he had been chief engineer and general manager since 1914. Collectively, those trail builders were moving ever closer to creating America's first through-trails.

Likewise, beginning at the turn of the century and continuing into the 1930s, hiking clubs were being organized throughout the Northeast. As those clubs came into existence, they brought forth other trail advocates who defended concepts much like MacKaye's. For example, during 1910 and 1911, William T. Howell of New York's Fresh Air Club defended the wilderness areas of the Hudson Highlands. Containing Bear Mountain and Harriman Park, that area was experiencing overuse pressures due to increased development of access roads and its roughly forty-mile proximity to New York City. Howell devoted himself with a MacKaye-like passion to preserving the wildness of the Highlands. Aware of this land's fragile and fading moment in history, he wrote passionately, "There is something more at stake here than the preservation of the scenery." He continued, "Some day, there will be none left. And then, a valuable species of citizen is going to grow extinct." Howell's plea to "keep out

Major William A. Welch

all foreign influences" falls directly into line with MacKaye's evolving concept for the entire Appalachian high country.

Certainly Vermont's Long Trail was a precursor to the Appalachian Trail. However, in 1916, well before the Long Trail reached its destination in Canada, U.S. Forester William Hall addressed the initial meeting of the New England Trail Conference with his prophetic hope of "completing a system of trails to traverse all the New England mountain ranges, and be linked ultimately with the southern Appalachians." In Laura and Guy Waterman's comprehensive treatment of Northeast hiking history, *Forest and Crag*, they assert, "This is the earliest known instance of someone's envisioning a foot trail extending up and down the entire Eastern seaboard — almost five years before the publication of Benton MacKaye's celebrated article on the Appalachian Trail." Throughout New England — spurred by trail builders, hiking clubs, and wilderness visionaries — fertile ground was being laid for MacKaye's grandiose plan. While MacKaye would father this singular vision, the early New England/New York hiking community prepared the stage upon which his Appalachian Trail project would soon premiere. The concept of an Appalachian ridgeline trail needed a voice; the project to create a through-trail along the Appalachian Mountains needed a founding father.

MacKaye's life was suddenly upended with the sudden death of his wife, Jessie Hardy "Betty" Stubbs, in April 1921. She took her life, after waiting for

*Jessie Hardy "Betty"
Stubbs MacKaye*

a train *en route* to an upstate sanitarium, by bolting from Grand Central Station and jumping into New York City's East River. He sought refuge in writing. At the insistence of friends, he retreated to the country farm of Charles Whitaker in northwestern New Jersey. Here, MacKaye began to formulate his vision for an Appalachian ridgeline trail. From those quiet sessions of writing for therapy, MacKaye first placed on paper a proposal titled, "Survey and Plan for an Outdoor Recreation System throughout the Appalachian Mountain Region."

Whitaker enthusiastically embraced MacKaye's proposal and invited another friend, Clarence Stein, then chairman of the committee on community planning for the Washington-based American Institute of Architects, to meet at Hudson Guild Farm, a nearby recreational and environmental education retreat for the inner-city poor, to discuss MacKaye's proposal. The July 10, 1921, meeting of those three provocative, regional thinkers was the incubator that launched MacKaye's article, "An Appalachian Trail: A Project in Regional Planning." Whitaker, as editor of the *Journal of the American Institute of Architects,* agreed to publish the article, and Stein agreed to assist MacKaye with the promotion of the Appalachian Trail project to his large circle of influential friends. And thus the Appalachian Trail project was born.

Over the next several years, MacKaye willingly filled the void in his life that was created through the loss of his wife by traveling up and down the East Coast, speaking to select groups of influential men, and gathering support for his Appalachian Trail project. He began in Cambridge, Massachusetts, by reconnecting with his "old woods teacher," Sturgis Pray, and another "old comrade," Allen Chamberlain. Chamberlain, a former Appalachian Mountain Club president, recommended to MacKaye that he next talk to Laurence L. Schmeckebier and Francois Mathes in Washington, D.C. Dr. Schmeckebier had a distinguished career in several U.S. government departments; Mathes worked for the Geological Survey and was an active member of the Sierra Club.

However, MacKaye next went to New York to reconnect with Whitaker and Stein and meet with Raymond Torrey, editor of a weekly outdoors column in the *New York Evening Post.* This connection proved instrumental in introducing the Appalachian Trail project to a broad audience of *Evening Post* readers, and it also led to meeting Major Welch, general manager of the New York–New Jersey Palisades Interstate Park. Finally, in the spring of 1922, MacKaye made his way to Washington, where he connected with "Schmeck" and Mathes and the U.S. Forest Service's Clinton Smith and Verne Rhoades. Other people of influence that MacKaye visited in what he called "the prenatal period of the Appalachian Trail" included Paul Fink in east Tennessee; Dr. H.S. Hedges of Charlottesville, Virginia; and Harlan P. Kelsey, who was working with Major Welch to establish eastern national parks as members of a federal commission that would become highly influential in A.T. development behind the scenes.

Harlean James is second from the right in both photographs. Above with managers of women's hotels (she converted them from failed boarding houses around the Capitol). Below at the 1937 ATC meeting in Gatlinburg, Tennessee, with Myron H. Avery at left and Marion Park at far right. In the center is Frederick F. Schuetz, ATC treasurer.

One vigorous, still going, and not forgotten lady.

Benton MacKaye, describing Harlean James

MacKaye's roster of key contacts during this period is noticeably devoid of women. However, as planning began for a meeting to give organizational structure to MacKaye's concept, one woman stepped into a position of influence. When the first "Appalachian Trail conference" met at the Raleigh Hotel in Washington in early March 1925, the widely acknowledged organizer of the meeting was Miss Harlean James, executive secretary of the American Planning and Civic Association. Although little has been written concerning her involvement in the Appalachian Trail project, Larry Anderson states in his definitive biography, *Benton MacKaye: Conservationist, Planner, and Creator of the Appalachian Trail,* that Harlean first demonstrated interest in the Trail project in 1923. An October 26-28, 1923, meeting was convened by MacKaye and the group led by Welch and Torrey (the Palisades Interstate Trail Conference, newly renamed the New York–New Jersey Trail Conference) at the Bear Mountain Inn. Harlean was among approximately thirty "not too serious people" that included a mix of planners from MacKaye's circle of friends, state foresters, conservationists, and hikers — all brought together to form an organization to give substance to his Appalachian Trail vision. Among their accomplishments at that 1923 meeting was the adoption of Major Welch's design of

the letter "A" having the crossbar superimposed with the letter "T" that has endured to this day as the official insignia of the Appalachian Trail. Plans were also laid for the convening of the organizational meeting that occurred in 1925 in Washington. As an attendee at the 1923 Bear Mountain Inn meeting and then as principal organizer of the 1925 meeting, Harlean James was in the middle of this early swirl of Trail activity — apparently captivated by the Trail concept and set on becoming a part of the Trail project.

Welch's first Trail marker

Born in Illinois, far from the Northeast's Appalachian region, Harlean James attended high school in Denver, Colorado, and completed her education with a bachelor's degree and postgraduate work from the University of Chicago and Columbia University, specializing in public relations. Early in her career, she held a variety of jobs, including serving as a court reporter in Honolulu, Hawaii, working her way up to become a sugar-company executive — a rare achievement for a woman in the corporate world of the early twentieth century. By 1921, as Benton MacKaye was formulating his plan for an Appalachian Trail, James was well-established as executive secretary of the American Planning and Civic Association. She has been described as erect in posture and dynamic in spirit, with a ruddy complexion and sparkling blue eyes. Attesting to her love of the outdoors, she once remarked, "There is nothing which makes you feel as far away from petty problems and seemingly insurmountable difficulties as perspectives from mountain tops over distant vistas." Thoughts such as that harken back to a basic premise of MacKaye's 1921 article that city dwellers find much-needed respite in wilderness. From her French Provincial Washington home at 2744 22nd Street N.W., James could gaze across to Rock Creek Park, an area she was known to frequent. She was also known to comment, "I send up a daily prayer that I may be vouchsafed the active use of my walking apparatus as long as I live." That James was attracted to the Appalachian Trail project seems only natural. And, once attracted, she confidently entered MacKaye's growing circle of influential men.

Additional brief mentions in Anderson's book reveal that Harlean James' association with the Trail project was not short-lived. In fact, as Trail construction proceeded, both Benton MacKaye and Myron Avery continued to consult with her.

In 1931, with President Herbert Hoover's plans for a mountaintop, scenic highway along the Appalachian range in Virginia's Shenandoah National Park moving into high gear, MacKaye sought the advice of Harlean James on how such parkways, which he perceived as intrusions into wilderness, could coexist with the Appalachian Trail.

Additionally, in 1945, she joined Avery in representing the Appalachian Trail Conference to address the Congress's Committee on Roads. Together, they provided testimony and offered endorsement of a bill proposing a national trails system and naming the Appalachian Trail as the first path to be included in the system — a bill proposed by Representative Daniel Hoch, an ATC board member before his one term in Congress.

Those two examples demonstrate Harlean James' long-term commitment to the Trail project. They also reveal a high level of confidence that MacKaye and Avery placed in her abilities to comprehend complex issues confronting the Trail project and future opportunities that could be unlocked by garnering political support. No wonder MacKaye described her in 1952 as "one vigorous, still going, and not forgotten lady."

When the Appalachian Trail conference convened at Washington's Hotel Raleigh on March 2, 1925, the array of speakers and the program reflected how powerful MacKaye's idea had grabbed official and public attention. As organizer, Harlean James brought together a "who's who" of state and federal foresters, state park officials, trail club officials, and National Park Service representatives to form the first structure by which the project would be advanced. Since this meeting is widely regarded as giving birth to the organization that would oversee MacKaye's Appalachian Trail project, Harlean James' presence is irrefutable evidence that women had a role in the Trail project from its beginnings.

At this meeting, the conference became a *bona fide* Conference organization, and Harlean James was elected secretary, a traditional female role but nonetheless a position on the very first board of directors. In many respects, the history of women in the Appalachian Trail project began with Harlean James and her service to the Appalachian Trail Conference (ATC). The presence of Harlean James at this meeting was also to serve as a hallmark of the role women would play in making MacKaye's dream a reality.

What we are doing here is building a lasting organization....

Myron H. Avery

Although MacKaye was not offered an official position on ATC's first board, he was given the title "field organizer," appropriately recognizing his on-going efforts to organize the field of people in key positions up and down the eastern seaboard that could transform his concept into trail on the ground. However, over the next few years, little progress was made toward actually getting trail built. In November 1927, the project got a tremendous boost when the Potomac Appalachian Trail Club (PATC) was formed in Washington. Various unsubstantiated stories within the Potomac club's archives tell of a young, energetic lawyer named Myron H. Avery, who was inspired by the current chairman of the ATC, Hartford, Connecticut, Judge Arthur Perkins, and then recruited to the project — or jumped in unasked himself, depending on the stories.

Whatever any past connection between Perkins and Avery, we can assume that it was more than fate that brought Avery to Washington to accept a position as an admiralty lawyer with the U.S. Shipping Board and subsequently led him to the old Metropolitan Bank Building on 15th Street N.W. on the evening of November 22, 1927. Here, Avery was joined by five other men (including early MacKaye contact L.L. Schmeckebier) who were equally inspired by reports from scouting parties that the cutting of a hiking trail along the Appalachian ridgeline in Virginia and West Virginia was indeed feasible. It was just the news they wanted to hear!

As these men selected a name for their new trail club and elected their first officers, including Avery as president, the task began of building trail through the central Appalachians. From his position as president, which he would hold for the next thirteen years, Avery relentlessly drove the Trail project to completion and earned his place beside Benton MacKaye as a founding father of the Appalachian Trail. Whatever club records may reveal, the net cast by MacKaye brought in Perkins and then Avery — both very good catches.

Although Harlean James played a key role in the initial meeting of the Appalachian Trail Conference, she was not present at the later organizational meeting of the PATC. But, like many other early volunteers — both men and women — she dedicated a significant amount of time and energy toward serving both organizations. She arranged for PATC and ATC to use space at 901 Union Trust Building, where her office was located, as joint headquarters. In occupying the same space and drawing from a very similar pool of volunteers, the activities of the Potomac club and the Trail Conference were often indistinguishable during those early years. That arrangement would continue until 1940, when PATC began renting office space at 1624 H Street, NW. Over time, the two agencies distinguished themselves through separate missions — PATC as a trail-building and trail-maintaining powerhouse and ATC as the national voice for the advancement, preservation, and promotion of the Appalachian Trail.

Harlean James was also instrumental in bringing other women into the Washington hiking scene and particularly into the membership of the Potomac club. For example, she invited Mary Jo Kempt, a member of her staff at the Planning and Civic Association, to join a PATC weekend excursion in February 1929. Mary Jo, in turn, invited Ruby Anderson, a coworker, along on another trip shortly after the February excursion, and afterward both Mary Jo and Ruby joined PATC. In those early years, Mary Jo and Ruby did much of the club's clerical work — typing letters, making telephone calls, taking trip reservations — often from their place of work and under the supervising eyes of Harlean James. A note within the November 1938 council meeting minutes of PATC, made by Avery, lightheartedly states that Miss Harlean James was *not* annoyed at the amount of time the telephone calls took from Ruby's working time during the day. Benton MacKaye would later affectionately describe Mary Jo and Ruby as Harlean's "gallant crew."

David Bates, in his history of the early years of the Potomac Appalachian Trail Club, *Breaking Trail in the Central Appalachians — a Narrative*, acknowledges that, within the first year of the formation of PATC, "There were people, many of the 'fair sex,' as was said then, who were willing to go out in the woods and do physical labor with considerable enthusiasm to help make a hiking trail on the crest of the Appalachians." In addition to James, Kempt, and Anderson, PATC records indicate that, in 1929, another woman, Dorothy Kemball, was invited by her cousins to join in a

Mary Jo Kempt in Washington's Glover Park with Myron Avery (right) in 1940. Landscape architect Howard Olmsted is at left.

Sunday hike. Despite her initial uncomfortable feeling of wearing knickers, which she considered "very wild" on a girl, especially on a Sunday, Dorothy also joined the club.

As over-all club membership continued to grow, so did the number of women members. Articles in local newspapers expounding the activities of the Potomac club helped to fuel the growth in membership and apparently offered a special appeal to women in the Washington area. Reportedly during these early years, women began showing their enthusiasm for club activities by turning out in equal numbers to the men, despite the fact that their membership base numbers were less than those for men. Oddly, *The Washington Herald* of November 2, 1930, carried a story on the activities of PATC that included the comment that "membership is restricted so that women never comprise more than 40 per cent of the membership, and keep the club on a "hard-boiled' basis." The restriction of a 60/40, men-to-women membership ratio was explained in club records as a strategy to ensure equal participation and a balance of companionship in club activities. This ratio, which was set by PATC's council at its September 18, 1930, meeting, was just as quickly abolished in March 1931. By the end of 1931, membership records showed 159 men and 113 women, or a 58/42 ratio — a modest two percentage-point rise in the number of women admitted to the club.

The attraction that the Appalachian Trail project held for women in these early years — as demonstrated by the Potomac Appalachian Trail Club records — is worthy of note. In club records and photographs, the women often appeared to band together on hikes and trail-cutting trips; however, occasionally, a lone woman would also appear to comfortably join an otherwise all-male group. Quite likely, the social climate of the nation's capital attracted young women with modern ideas, while the economic climate that resulted from the availability of steady-paying government jobs provided sufficient financial stability for young women to seek after-work activities beyond the reach of their factory-working and work-at-home peers during this decade of the Great Depression. Within this setting, a class of young, well-educated, government-employed women enjoyed free time in the evenings and weekends, as well as occasional vacations. Those young women who gravitated to the Trail project obviously wanted to fill their leisure time with activities very different from the traditional female activities of their mothers' generation.

Spent night — a very cold night in the Fells Cottage... a good fire, but beds all very cold in spite of blankets which we brot from home... Never have seen the Skyland Drive — esp. the north end so beautiful — a very satisfactory trip.

Kathryn Fulkerson, describing a 1936 Skyland Drive trip

Before long, a corps of women was spending time each evening at PATC and ATC's joint office, typing letters, publishing club notices, and preparing articles to submit to newspapers and magazines informing the public of the Appalachian Trail project. And, each weekend, they banded together with other adventure-seeking women and men, boarded buses and trains, and headed to the nearby Blue Ridge to blaze trail, cut brush, cook over campfires, and bunk down under a forested canopy.

Just as MacKaye postulated in his 1921 article, those busy workers from Monday to noon Saturday were seeking solitude and solace in the Appalachian ridge-top wilderness. And among their ranks were a growing number of modern, high-spirited women. Kathryn Fulkerson, Marian Lapp, and Jewell Glass, who joined PATC in the early 1930s, are perfect examples. Described as "young professional women, well-educated, and permanently employed in good jobs" and as "dressed in the latest outdoor fashions," those three women became regular volunteers handling the office work of PATC and avid participants in the club's outdoor activities.

Kathryn Fulkerson worked in the Justice Department, where she was known to refuse promotions that would require overtime work and infringe upon her leisure time to participate in Trail activities. From 1936 to 1942, she was PATC's general secretary, and, with Marian Lapp, served as the first Trail overseers for the southern Maryland section of the A.T., from Crampton Gap to Weverton. Seldom did this pair miss any club activities throughout the 1930s. Together with Jewell Glass, they roomed at the Ethelhurst Apartments on 15th Street NW. All three women had a tremendous dedication to PATC and the Trail project, as evidenced by Fulkerson's and Lapp's donation of their now-Trailside house, "Highacre," at Harpers Ferry, West Virginia, to the Potomac club, and Glass' donation of her vacation home, "Glass House," to the club, also.

Another attraction for women may have been the organization, planning, and structure that the clubs provided for its activities, which offered adventure tempered with somewhat expected outcomes. During the 1920s and 1930s, travel from downtown Washington to the nearby Blue Ridge routinely presented an adventure in transportation and, once on the mountain, an outdoor experience in a land that was in many ways unmapped and untramped. Work trips and hikes in the central Appalachians could prove to be wild, indeed!

Frank Schairer, PATC's supervisor of trails in these early years and a key Avery lieutenant, described the challenges trail workers faced when leaving the relative comforts of Washington to blaze and cut the Trail. In a 1942 interview, he stated,

> "You had to go to Harpers Ferry, drive quite a distance on a dirt road to Millville, and get a mountaineer out of his cabin to take you across the river by a hand-operated ferry…. I remember one trip in February, we started on Sunday morning, and it was nearly twelve o'clock noon before we arrived at Keys Gap. We were working near the Deer Lick, and the Trail was really bad. By the time we walked to the Deer Lick, it was three-thirty or a quarter to four, and we figured we had only fifteen minutes to work before we had to start back. It started to sleet, and the sole came off my shoe, and there I was. We put in fifteen minutes of hard work and had to race back to Keys Gap before dark."

One early female adventurer who quite comfortably accepted those types of outdoor challenges was Marion Park, who joined PATC in 1934, served as assistant editor of PATC's newsletter, *the Bulletin,* under Mary Jo Kempt, and later replaced Harlean James as secretary of ATC — a position she would hold for fifteen years. Marian seldom missed a club outing and was often seen in the early years following Myron Avery on the Trail and taking notes on distances and conditions, as Avery pushed his measuring wheel along the proposed trail routes.

Through their membership in trail clubs, those early Appalachian Trail women were seeking not only adventures but also companionship and good times. Leadership within the Potomac club, like the leadership of many of the maintaining clubs, recognized that having a genuine good time was a key to growing a dependable core of trail workers. Trail-blazing and trail-cutting were difficult tasks, but, when tempered with social activities such as square dances,

Marion Park, at left recording excursions-committee meeting notes in February and below heading out from the 1939 ATC meeting at Daicey Pond in Maine for a trail-wheeling trip with Myron Avery.

talent shows, and camping excursions, club rosters grew. And, as new recruits became more involved in the club's activities, they soon found friendship with other like-minded people — quite often with the opposite sex. Camaraderie on the trail often led to lasting friendships, and many friendships blossomed into romance. Quite possibly, such friendships and romances may have been nurtured by trail settings that, by all accounts, lacked the social "properness" of the city or the office.

For example, Mary Jo Kempt joined PATC in 1929 and, in 1935, married fellow club member Charlie Williams. Additionally, as recounted in Bates' *Breaking Trail in the Central Appalachians*, the following met and married during their time with the Potomac club: Andy Anderson and Edna Thomas in 1933; Egbert Walker and Dorothy Kemball in 1936; Joe Winn and Joan Roetzer also in 1936; Bill Mersch and Ruth Brown in 1938; Ken Boardman and Vivian Robb, Frank Schairer and Ruth Naylor, Leo Scott and Guinevere Feckler in 1939; and Herman Noltz

A Potomac A.T. Club bus trip in 1928

and Ruby Anderson in 1944. Bates explains this trend as "perhaps quite naturally, as members had the same interests and were with each other on many weekends, often under the stress of bad weather, and poor accommodations, and hard physical work under difficult conditions, which really gave one an insight into the character of one's companions." Such conditions could quickly reveal various levels of compatibility — or incompatibility — between members of the opposite sex. Experiencing harsh weather, losing one's way on poorly marked trail sections, or pushing automobiles out of unexpected mud or snow, created strong bonds among club members who actually enjoyed such trail hardships — bonds that often lead to lasting friendships and then to matrimony.

Conversely, not all women who joined a trail club were looking for sheer good fun — or even romance — in the outdoors. That is evidenced by membership in PATC's notorious Dirty Dozen. Known as the "trouble-shooting shock troops" of the club, that group of men and women took on the most difficult sections of trail-cutting and trail-maintaining in the central Appalachians. Among their ranks were Mary Jo Kempt, Ruby Anderson, Vivian Robb, Edna Thomas, and Betty Merwarth. Their interests went beyond fun and adventure, as they worked beside their male counterparts to do the hardest Trail work. Those women shared in the prestige that came with being identified as honestly earning membership into the Dirty Dozen. They provide evidence that, from its earliest days, the Appalachian Trail project attracted a special group of women who found personal satisfaction in the physically demanding work of trail-building and enjoyment in being in the company of like-minded and like-motivated men and women.

Times on the Appalachian Trail meant hard, physical work, often in conjunction with the discomforts of cold, rain, or heat. Although early club records reveal that women were most often involved in the Appalachian Trail project in traditional female leadership positions, such as club secretaries and corresponding secretaries, and most often were found performing traditional female tasks, such as cleaning shelters or cooking around a campfire, women were welcomed from the very early days of the A.T. project to join in the hard work of trail-cutting and in the hardships often experienced during activities such as hiking and camping. And, while women's membership certainly added to the appeal of the club's social activities, such as square dances, talent shows, recognition dinners, and song fests, their membership became increasing important to the club's ability to perform its basic function of building and maintaining the Appalachian Trail. In short, women held their own place alongside men, as MacKaye's vision for a ridgeline footpath along the Appalachian Mountains moved ever closer to becoming a reality.

It is here among that league of early Appalachian Trail women that we find one woman with the visionary talent of Benton MacKaye and the unwavering determination of Myron Avery. She was intelligent, independent, and adventuresome. She possessed organizational skills, loved the outdoors, and thrived on hard work. Above all, she embraced the Trail project. Her name is Jean Stephenson. And, in telling the story of her long association with the Appalachian Trail project, we pay tribute to all of those early women trail blazers.

Men and women in 1935 enhance the original 1933 Katahdin summit sign and cairn.

Myron Avery and Jean Stephenson atop Sentinel Mountain in Maine, on a hike after the 1939 ATC meeting she organized.

Dear Mr. York, Mrs. York, Junior and Phyllis,

I have been intending ever since I reached home to write a note just to tell you how much we enjoyed our stay at your camps....

Jean Stephenson letter of October 21, 1939

CHAPTER 3

JEAN STEPHENSON

1892–1979

After months of preparation, the Appalachian Trail Conference's 1939 general meeting at Daicey Pond, at the foot of Katahdin west of Millinocket, Maine, had come, gone, and achieved an overwhelming success. Jean Stephenson's letter to the Yorks of Twin Pines Camps is bittersweet, with a pervading undertone of longing for the mountains, lakes, and primitive hunting camps of Maine. Upon her return to Washington, Jean most likely could not help but reflect upon how starkly different her present surroundings were compared to the remote setting of the Yorks' lakeside camp. One can almost hear Jean sigh deeply as she closes her letter with words of acceptance for an uncertain future:

"When I got back to Washington, I found that war had broken out in Europe. As I am with the Navy Department, you can readily imagine that my time is more than taken up and the consequence is that I see already it will not be possible for me to have my winter visit with you this winter. Possibly another year...."

Officially as chair of the ATC's reservation committee for the 1939 meeting, Jean began writing letters to Mr. and Mrs. York in September 1938, a full eleven months before the group of primarily Washington hikers would converge on the Yorks' Twin Pines Camps, just outside the boundary of the new Maine state park to be named after Percival Baxter. Their camps offered a perfect setting for those expected to attend the meeting and particularly for the hikes being planned as part of the week's activities.

Meetings would be held from Friday afternoon, August 18, through Saturday, August 20. Sunday would feature a hike to Sentinel Mountain followed by a hike to Double Top Mountain on Monday. The high point of the week would be an overnight trip to Katahdin, staying at Katahdin Lake Camps. The Yorks' Twin Pine Camps offered eleven rustic cabins with occupancy from two to twelve, a dining room with seating capacity of sixty-four, and a field for tenting — making it an ideal base camp for the 1939 event.

Jean, as reservations chairperson (and *de facto* meeting chair), immediately applied her organizational skills and seemingly unbounded energies to make sure the accommodations, meals, meetings, hikes, and all other planned events ran like clockwork.

Soon, a constant stream of letters was relayed back and forth from Jean's typewriter to the Yorks and a variety of other Maine hunting camp owners (Jasper Hayes of Buck Horn Camp, William Myshrall of White Horse Camps, and Oliver Cobb of Katahdin Lake Camps) and also bus driver Harry Hasey. Mail delivery in that part of Maine was often slow and uncertain. Many of these inland folk noted in their letters that they were staying in camp for the winter with no intentions of traveling into town for their mail, and thus further correspondence "will be rather uncertain for the next three to four months." Jean's decision to begin the planning well in advance of the event proved to be both necessary and wise.

Throughout those months of planning, a letter would occasionally arrive in the Washington club office from Myron Avery, who was then serving his eighth year as chairman of the ATC and was soon to complete his twelfth year as president of the Potomac Appalachian Trail Club. Having recently accepted a war-related position as special assistant to the U.S. attorney and relocating his family to New York City, Avery was dealing with the challenges of leading ATC and PATC from afar. His letters, often handwritten in a distinctive script, were full of reminders to Jean of additional arrangements to be made for the upcoming meeting. Avery and Stephenson were masters of letter-writing, an indispensable skill during the early years of the Appalachian Trail project, and especially during the months leading up to such an event as the 1939 meeting, at a time when he and park benefactor Percival Baxter were at intense logger-heads. In their stream of letters, Stephenson would recount details, and Avery would issue directives. Together, plans for the 1939 meeting moved forward.

As a native of Maine, Avery had a very special fondness for its high peaks — especially Katahdin — and, as president of the PATC since its founding in 1927, he made week-long excursions and work trips to Maine a regular event for the club in the mid-to-late 1930s, putting the A.T. fully on the ground in his home state. With each visit, Myron's love of the Maine woods spread in-fectiously among his fellow members of PATC, including Jean, who also were the founding members of the Maine Appalachian Trail Club just a few years earlier.

Each year, club members anxiously awaited an announcement from Avery that he again would be leading a trip to this magical place that had been desig-nated as the northern terminus of the Appalachian Trail. Avery and his fellow PATC/MATC members undoubtedly had influenced the selection of Maine's Daicey Pond as the site for this meeting, and they applied their knowledge and first-hand experience of the area's hiking trails, camps, and local guides to planning the event. With Avery simultaneously holding the position of chair-man of ATC and president of PATC, swaying the selection of the meeting site to Maine would have been quite easy.

And, although the demands of his position as an admiralty lawyer with the U.S. Navy Shipping Board, temporarily assigned to the Justice Department in New York, required frequent travel, especially with the ominous events occur-ring throughout Europe, Avery maintained close contact with Jean and other club volunteers as planning continued for their 1939 meeting.

The evening of October 21, 1939, a month after Daicey Pond, was typical of many evenings for Jean as she sat at a typewriter at 1624 H Street, NW — around a corner off Lafayette Park across from the White House — writing her much-delayed letter to the Yorks, thanking them for accommodations, meals, and other kindnesses offered during the 1939 meeting.

At this Washington location, where the Potomac club rented an office and shared space with the ATC, Jean was one of a small, tight-knit corps of vol-unteers who were busy many evenings — and occasional Saturdays — doing the business of both trail organizations, such as answering telephones, typing letters, preparing trail maps and guidebooks, writing news releases, and planning club events. Government workers by day, those volunteers formed one of the first "Trail families" as they committed themselves to doing the work of running PATC and ATC.

Among the first letters Jean penned to Mr. York regarding plans for the 1939 meeting was one written on the evening of September 20, 1938 — the contents of which reveal much about her dedication to all things Trail-related. The letter is remarkable for its length — a full eight typewritten pages — and for its detail. In her usual super-efficient manner, Jean was setting forth the arrangements for the Conference meeting. Here she outlines the meeting's schedule of events, arrangements for cabins and tents, transportation by private car and train, dining-room seating, fees for each service, and even bed assignments. Her letter closes with somewhat diplomatic, but specific instruction to Mr. York and his workers to clean out certain trails between Twin Pine Camps and Katahdin "so that we may show these people what standard woods trail should be" and to also "create a good impression on your guests." Furthermore, she instructs Mr. York that an extra wash basin was to be placed in each cabin, buckets of hot water delivered each morning, and extra portable toilets placed in the tenting field. Jean performed the duties of chair of the reservation committee for ATC's ninth meeting with great seriousness; her attention to every detail would ensure its success.

And now, with the Maine trip a fond memory, Jean foreshadows in her October 1939 thank-you letter to the Yorks a very uncertain future for herself and her fellow Trail workers. Her recollections of the days spent at Twin Pines Camps and on the surrounding lakes, trails, and high peaks are filled with an obvious longing to return to the Maine woods. As she laments that it will be some time before she can return to those beloved north woods, the uncertainties of war not only force a cancellation of her winter plans but also threaten to separate her from the camaraderie of Trail friends that she has come to enjoy. Maine hiking with her A.T. friends made for a perfect week — and she knew not when experiences such as those of the 1939 meeting would be repeated.

For Jean and her fellow volunteers who formed this early family of A.T. workers, the lights would continue to burn weekday evenings in their H Street office, and Trail camaraderie would continue to knit them together as friends, sons, daughters, mothers, and fathers were called to serve their country. In that series of letters from September 1938 to October 1939, we are introduced to a multitalented woman wed to the Appalachian Trail — its organizational structure, its physical demands, its hiking community, and, most of all, its sheer beauty. Her life story forms an important, early chapter in the history of the Appalachian Trail project.

More and more for those of us whose fate it is to live in cities are realizing that really to live, to continue to enjoy life, to savour [sic] experiences as they come, it is necessary to keep in touch with Nature.... And more and more we are turning to the mountains to recapture that restfulness and peace that is essential if we are to continue to live normal unworried lives.

"The Appalachian Trail — What Is It?" by Jean Stephenson

TO ESCAPE CIVILITY

Perched upon a rock among the Catoctin Mountains of Maryland (see page 52), Jean Stephenson appears thoughtful and calculating. A trail map is spread across her knees; pen and paper are in her hands. That pose was typical of Jean, whose hikes were seldom mere walks in the woods. Yes, she wrote poetry about her mountain experiences, and she clearly enjoyed hiking. But more than being a trail walker, Jean gave purpose to her hikes. While walking in the Maine woods, she most often carried a paint can and brush to freshen the white blazes on trees and rocks that mark the pathway of the Appalachian Trail. And, as we see her here, Jean characteristically carried pen and notepaper to meticulously record trail locations, distances, and conditions. Jean was a person of detail. Her notes were clearly written; her measurements precisely recorded.

We can only imagine her hiking companions patiently waiting nearby, knowing that her notes, once carefully transcribed into newsletter articles, guidebooks or maps, would provide current trail information to many fellow hikers. Jean had a passion for those high hills, just as she also had a passion for exactness. She sees herself as someone whose words can lead others to those hills, where the experience will inspire them — as it did her — to dedicate themselves to the preservation of those special places. The emotions expressed in her simple poetry and the detail in her trail notes form the basis for Jean's ability to lead others into the Appalachian Trail movement. Should she look up from her notes, Jean's gaze would be cast far across mountaintops and rolling valleys, offering a perspective not unlike her expansive, forty-seven-year involvement with the Appalachian Trail.

Jean Stephenson was born on August 29, 1892, in Waco, Texas, the daughter of Edwin Napier Stephenson and Mattie James Baker. At an early age, Jean and her family moved to Massachusetts and from there to other locations throughout New England, as well as Chicago, Illinois; Ithaca, New York; and Philadelphia, Pennsylvania. As a result of those frequent family moves, Jean did not have a typical public education, but rather she was educated by a series of private teachers to the academic equivalent of a master's degree.

Throughout years of schooling, Jean trained as an accountant, editor, and lawyer with a special interest in history. From 1913 to 1914, she studied accounting at Cornell University, followed by a stint from 1914 to 1918 as assistant to the university's treasurer. After relocating to Washington in November 1918, she worked as an accountant in the U.S. Navy bureau of supplies and accounts, holding a variety of positions through 1950. The titles she assumed during this time reflect ever-increasing responsibilities: accountant from 1918 to 1924; technical advisor to Naval Claims Commission, 1925 to 1926; editor, 1926 to 1942; director of publications division, 1942 to 1949; and special assistant for publications to the chief of the bureau, 1949 to 1950.

While working for the Navy, Jean continued her academic studies, earning four law degrees from Washington's National University Law School by age forty-three: doctor of jurisprudence, master of laws, master of patent law, and doctor of juridical science. In 1929, she was admitted to the District of Columbia Bar, and, in 1931, Jean lectured on parliamentary law at National University, which would merge into George Washington University in the mid-1950s. Her academic achievements bear witness to her intelligence, but any career ambitions she may have had to practice law never materialized. Rather, Jean settled in for a long career with the Navy that would provide her with both a secure income and ample personal time to pursue other interests. She soon connected with a group of government workers who routinely escaped the civility of Washington to enjoy weekend forays in the nearby Shenandoahs. Jean gravitated toward this group, enjoying their camaraderie, and soon sharing their passion for mountain wilderness. As she settled into her job with the Navy, her leisure interests were directed more and more toward her newfound interest in hiking.

"Unselfish, enthusiastic and energetic, she was an inspiration to all who worked with her."

Breaking Trail in the Central Appalachians, **by David Bates**

FINDING A PERFECT FIT

The year 1933 marked the beginning of Jean's Appalachian Trail years. For a group of young professional Washingtonians, the metropolitan bus and train system provided a reliable means of escaping the city on weekends for trail-cutting work trips and hiking excursions in the nearby mountains of Maryland and Virginia. Jean became a regular participant in those activities, enjoying both the social life and vigorous outdoor exercise.

Jean was sponsored into membership of the Potomac Appalachian Trail Club in 1933, the same year the club welcomed two other single women, Marion Park and Anna Jespersen. Also coming to PATC in the 1930s were Kathryn Fulkerson, Ann Michener, Mary Jo Kempt, Marian Lapp, Jewell Glass, and Harlean James. This was a special group of women — single, working, independent, and ready for outdoor adventures.

In the Potomac club, those women found a social climate quite different from their Monday-through-Friday working environments. Here they could sport the latest fashions for women in the outdoors — felt hats or printed bandannas, cotton pants, and sturdy walking shoes — and relax into roles less feminine and more equal to their male hiking companions. Dorothy Kemball, who appeared wearing knickers as a guest on her first hike with the club in 1928, reported feeling "very wild" and yet comfortable enough with the group to join the club later that year. Dorothy was not alone in her enjoyment of the club's organized trips, and, by 1930, club leadership observed that women often comprised more than fifty percent of the participants in club's activities.

Explained as an effort to provide for better companionship between the sexes, a restriction was placed on PATC's membership in September 1930, requiring that females comprise no more than forty percent of the total club roster. Whatever the reason, the restriction was short-lived. By March 1931 — just three months later — the council reversed its decision. When Jean was sponsored into membership in 1933, there would be no counting of the sexes. She was in, and she stayed.

For those early women members, the organizational structure of the club meant that excursions into mountain areas at first unfamiliar to them were well-planned. They could participate as adventurers, enjoying just the right amount of wilderness challenge in the company of well-seasoned club leaders. For several years, however, their level of participation in hikes was somewhat restricted as announced in the club's *Bulletin*: "[G]irls were given class B trips, as they were not so difficult." Even that unofficial restriction was soon forgotten. While club activities often included some degree of unpredictability — changes in weather, impassable roads, unexpected stream crossings — the planning and preparedness that went into each club activity afforded these women a reasonable amount of safety. Jean and other female hikers quickly embraced the hardships of rain, cold, poor road conditions, poorer trail conditions, and the absence of maps, fresh water, and sanitation. To them, their introduction to PATC activities was sheer fun.

During those early years, membership in the Potomac club was regulated through a set of procedures that required applicants to go on at least two trips, club-sponsored or private, and to be sponsored into membership by at least two members. The club was looking for new members who demonstrated a degree of independence, but also compatibility and sportsmanship, with above all the willingness to endure outdoor hardships. New members also were expected to share in the work load of cutting and maintaining trail. As early member Anna Jespersen stated so well in David Bates' *Breaking Trail in the Central Appalachians*, "PATC was not a snob organization…but it could not afford to be burdened with members who could not accept foul weather, chiggers, ticks, poison ivy, and other hazards of the outdoors in good grace. Also, the trail had to be maintained…."

At the time Jean joined the PATC, membership was at 267 and the club treasury boasted a modest balance of $132.74. Much had been accomplished since the club was formed in 1927 by a group of six men determined to infuse some "might and muscle" into a somewhat stagnated movement to create a long trail along the ridgeline of America's Appalachian Mountains. Under the leadership of founding member and President Myron Avery, PATC quickly was established as a forceful, maintaining member club of the Appalachian Trail Conference.

An admiralty lawyer, Avery applied his passion for the hardships of outdoor life to his unmatched endurance for trail-blazing and trail-building and his remarkable talent to recruit the right people to complete the trail in the central and southern Appalachians and ensure its completion from Maine to Georgia. Perhaps it was Myron Avery's relentless efforts to recruit workers from the various government departments that reached Jean in the Navy's bureau of supplies and accounts and drew her into PATC. Regardless, Jean found a perfect fit at PATC for her growing love of the outdoors and newfound interest in the Appalachian Trail project.

Charlie Williams, who would later marry Mary Jo Kempt, described one club trip in the 1930s in these simple words: "We had the best times." The spirit of those early trail workers is well-documented by David Bates:

> *The enthusiasm shown by members in getting groups together each weekend and going out to open new or to clear out old trail was what really kept things moving. Dedication, love of the outdoors, the goal of having a trail all the way from Maine to Georgia — whatever the motivating factors were — they went out in numbers each weekend…and got the job done. And had fun!*

Among Jean's earliest contributions to the Potomac club was heading up a group of sixteen women to make blue-jean mattress covers for the club's shelters along the Appalachian Trail, a task considered typical for women, and maintaining with Marion Park a side trail of the A.T. from Meadow Spring and Buck Hollow trails, not so typical for women.

As Myron and his small band of trail-builders continued to place more miles of trail on the ground in the central Appalachians, it became necessary to divide the completed footpath into manageable sections and assign "overseers" to perform regular maintenance on each section. By July 1934 — after being a club member for just one year — Jean became acting secretary of the overseers. Frank Schairer, as supervisor of trails, now depended upon Jean to communicate to each overseer the need to keep their section of trail open. For example, in July 1934, Frank wrote to overseer H. S. Krider of Cherrydale, Virginia — who with a group of Boy Scouts was maintaining a section of trail between Turners and Crampton gaps — that, as he would be traveling away from Washington for a month and a half, Mr. Krider was to report directly to Jean on the present condition of that section of trail and future plans to go out and clear it.

Jean fell right into the role of writing streams of letters urging workers to visit their assigned sections, to stay ahead of summer growth, and to return club tools promptly. Not one to miss an opportunity to find out about activities that could impact the Trail, she would often include in her letters to the overseers subtle inquiries, such as questioning them about any road-building by the Civilian Conservation Corps. Acutely aware that this type of activity could lead to a relocation of the Trail, Jean would pass the overseers' information on to Frank, who then wrote to the appropriate authorities with the confidence of knowing the conditions on the ground. Thus, from her modest involvements of stitching mattress covers and maintaining one side trail, Jean began to establish a reputation within the club as a person of detail and organization, with a clear willingness to apply those skills to advance the Appalachian Trail project.

Within a short time, Jean's interest in the A.T. project grew to encyclopedic proportions and spread into other areas. Described by one club member as "one of the brightest persons I have ever known," Jean also was often credited with having her oddities.

Filing cabinets began to fill her Washington apartment from floor to ceiling, their contents reflecting her extensive knowledge of the Appalachian Trail as well as her membership in the Daughters of the American Revolution, League of American Penwomen, National Genealogical Society, American Association for State and Local History, National Society of Colonial Dames of America, and numerous other societies.

Her first official position in the Potomac club was to serve as chairman of the trail history committee. In that position, she regularly contributed articles to the club's *Bulletin* under the heading "Historical Ramblings." Writing for each edition of the *Bulletin* offered Jean the chance to use some of her academic skills, such as research, composition, and editing. Her articles covered a variety of topics, all with a connection to the Appalachian Mountains and having such titles as "The Indians and Early Settlers of the Cumberland Valley" (April 1935); "Skyland Before 1900" (July 1935); "From Browns Gap to Rockfish Gap" (October 1936); "Winter in the Pennsylvania Hills — 1736" (January 1937); "Why Is It Called That?" (April 1938); and "Pennsylvania Names" (October 1938).

Here Jean also became a great storyteller, giving the Appalachian Trail project an historical context and a cultural identity. The readers of her articles quite often were familiar with the places she was describing — Dark Hollow, Sexton Knoll, Rockfish Gap — as they had most likely hiked to those places many times on club excursions. But, did they know the histories behind those Appalachian landmarks? Jean's articles introduced club members to the Appalachian mountain people whose customs, industries, and adventures were imprinted upon these Appalachian places. Through her writings, their hidden stories were revealed.

For example, in "Skyland Before 1900," Jean tells the story of a section of northern Virginia's Blue Ridge that was destined to become Shenandoah National Park. Her growing interest in historical research of the Appalachians is obvious as she begins this article, and many others, by harkening back to the early 1700s, when the first white men attempted to occupy that hill country. In this article, Jean rambled on until approximately midarticle, where she introduced George Pollock of the Stony Man Mining Company. In recounting the story of Mr. Pollock's son, G. Freeman Pollock, founder of the mountain resort, Skyland, Jean offered her readers the story behind that popular destination for many Potomac Club excursions. In doing so, future club excursions to Skyland took on a new perspective — one made much richer through Jean's attention to every detail in the history of Skyland and many other Appalachian places.

In the same article, Jean told the story of Thornton Gap and Mary's Rock, both popular destinations on PATC hikes:

> Thornton Gap preserves the name of Francis Thornton, who as early as 1733 built a home in F.T. Valley (so called from his initials) and whose land ran far up the hollow. The story goes that he [Francis Thornton] brought his bride, the beautiful Mary Savage from Westmoreland County…and one day they rode to the top of the Great Pass Mountain, then climbed the rocks on the

summit, from which he pointed out his land and presented it to her...because
she was the first white woman to climb the mountain, the rock pile on top was
called after her, 'Mary's Rock.'

Similarly, in her April 1938 article, "Why is it called that?" Jean employed a writing style that resembled folklore with an academic twist. Again, she offered her A.T. readers something special — an interesting rambling sure to be recalled the next time club members hiked through the central Appalachians. She writes, "The names of the persons form an epitome of history of the region," and, she concludes, "Their names are on the mountainside, ye cannot wash them out." As the Appalachian region became a land that Jean would grow to know as a hiker, its people and places became the subjects of her writing for club newsletters. In short, she was becoming captivated by the genealogy of the Appalachian region, that is, the tracing of the ancestry of these ancient mountains, gaps, waterways, and physical features.

Through Jean's early writings in the club newsletters, the Appalachian Trail takes on a history of place *and* establishes its place in history. Yes, it is a wilderness footpath, but it also offers a window into the past history of the Appalachian Mountain region and the folk who inhabited it.

During those early trail-building years of the 1930s, the Appalachian Trail project presented a contrast of cultures. PATC trail workers dressed differently and spoke differently from the simple-living folk of the mountains, hollows, and gaps where the Trail was being built. And, many were government workers, mistrusted by the Appalachian Mountain families and unwelcome in their secluded mountain lands. Trail work could be hampered easily by the local mountain families who were quick to regard city folk with suspicion and occasionally contempt. Such feelings were deep-rooted and could lead to violence.

David Bates, in *Breaking Trails in the Central Appalachians,* described an incident that occurred during a club hike in May 1930 to Hazel Mountain. A large group of fifty-five hikers had divided into two groups, thirty heading up Buck Hollow and the remainder visiting Hazel Mountain Church and School. As the first group rested on Old Rag following lunch at the summit, some noticed smoke rising from below and on both sides of the mountain. Calmness prevailed as the group was led off the mountain, and all returned safely to the bus. There was little doubt that this fire was set, confirming that those who lived in these remote regions regarded bus-loads of city hikers as unwelcome intruders.

Encounters between mountain folk and trail workers were not always filled with apprehension and mistrust. For example, many stories were told within the Potomac club of Frank Schairer's acceptance by the Shenandoah mountain folks. As supervisor of trails from 1932 to 1943, Frank led many work trips into the Shenandoah area, where his willingness to drink their moonshine, join them in hunting trips, and avoid interference with their habits and customs, earned the trust of the Shenandoah families. Trail workers such as Frank, who showed respect, acceptance, and understanding of the mountain folks, were better able to advance the Trail project and even recruit strong, solid workers from among the mountain families to assist in building the trail and its shelters.

Unexpected good times were also shared between PATC club members and the mountain families, as recounted by Kathryn Fulkerson in an early issue of the *Bulletin*. Apparently, Frank and three other men were singing around a campfire in Smoot Meadow late one night after a day of trail building when a group of mountain folk became an appreciative audience and even invited them back to their cabin to "sing for Granny" and have some refreshments. Then, the following October, when a fairly large group of club members went to inspect the new section of Trail, they found the mountain families had prepared a campfire and set up log benches in anticipation of another group sing-along. Certainly showing an acceptance of mountain folkways could prove advantageous to these Washington trail workers as they scouted, marked, and built the trail in what would become Shenandoah National Park.

However, by the mid-1930s, dramatic changes had occurred in the Shenandoah landscape and in the families that inhabited the region. In Jean's October 1936 article, "From Brown's Gap to Rockfish Gap," she writes about these mountain people and their changing landscape — blighted chestnut trees, dwindling game, and increased road-building. A short announcement titled, "Shenandoah National Park Formally Dedicated" follows her article. President Franklin D. Roosevelt officially dedicated the new park on July 3, 1936, but many details were missing from this brief announcement. Six thousand three hundred acres inhabited by the mountain families had been acquired by the state of Virginia, two hundred ninety-three mountain families were placed under a federally funded program to relocate beyond the established park boundaries, and a few elderly inhabitants were either allowed to remain in their mountain homes for their remaining days or were placed in the state welfare program.

In light of those events, Jean's articles became more than historical ramblings; they were documentaries of mountain places and mountain people undergoing dramatic changes. Jean's "Historical Ramblings" were one way of preserving the history of a quickly vanishing mountain way of life.

One works to create something for others to enjoy. Service is given unselfishly to clear trails, build shelters, measure trails, prepare directions, make maps and signs, write guides and other books, experiment with equipment, and put in hour after hour in routine office work and the myriad tasks that must be done on the Trail and away from it, if the Trail is to continue to exist.

"The Appalachian Trail — What Is It?" by Jean Stephenson

ADVOCATING FOR THE TRAIL

Throughout the 1930s and 1940s, Jean took on an amazing variety of positions within the Potomac club: trail history chair, 1933-34 and 1936; publicity committee chair, 1938; guidebook editor, 1939-1947; overseer of trails secretary, 1940-41; headquarters committee chair, 1941-48; and trail overseer for Ashby Gap, Meadow Spring, and Buck Hollow, 1942. And, as early as October 1934, Jean's volunteer work — both in the office and on the trail — began to stretch beyond the Washington-based Potomac club into the Appalachian Trail Conference. This was not unusual, since the Washington club and the Conference shared space within Harlean James' office during those early years. Intertwining of those two organizations was demonstrated most clearly by the one man who for many years headed both — the charismatic Myron Avery, seven years Jean's senior.

Avery was born in Lubec, Maine, but his career as an admiralty lawyer brought him to Washington, D.C., where he helped initiate the effort to form a hiking club dedicated to the task of building the central section of the Appalachian Trail. Like Jean, he would end up dedicating his life to the effort.

Myron's involvement in the trail project began in 1927 as founding president of the PATC, where his energies were concentrated on trail-building in the central Appalachians. By 1931, after the death of Judge Arthur Perkins, he was elected chairman of the ATC with responsibilities for overseeing trail building from Maine to Georgia. Likewise, Jean's service to the trail project quickly broadened beyond the Washington and central Appalachian areas.

Myron Avery and Jean Stephenson shared a commitment not only to the routine administrative tasks, such as writing letters, guidebooks, articles, and reports, but also to building, maintaining, and advocating for the Trail. Myron — as the emboldened, determined, and single-minded trail-builder — most often was found sporting a sleeveless dark "muscle" shirt, a tin cup clipped to his belt, and pushing his measuring wheel over the Appalachian ridgeline. In contrast, Jean was often seen in cotton pants with fashionable double buttons, crisp shirt fastened at the neck with a scarf, and hair delicately pulled back from her face.

Although an avid and accomplished hiker, Jean is quite often portrayed at a desk in a serious editor-in-chief pose, as she worked to transcribe Avery's trail notes and measurements into guidebooks, maps, newsletter articles, and feature stories. Their portrayed relationship was one of a mutually respectful, honest, and successful partnership that often placed Jean in a leading-from-behind position. Close examination of their written correspondences reveals, to the contrary, that their relationship was forged from a shared intensity to build the Appalachian Trail and the organizational structure necessary to sustain it. Neither would be denied these goals.

One of their earliest joint efforts was to push for national recognition for the Appalachian Trail. Knowing that the success of the A.T. depended not only on the dedication of trail workers but also on gaining widespread recognition for the project, Jean and Myron worked together to attract the attention of well-known publications, such as *National Geographic* magazine. Jean's persistence in dealing with the magazine's staff is evidenced in her letter dated October 11, 1934, to a Dr. William J. Showalter. Her communication begins by giving accolades to Avery's trail work and describing him as "the only person who has actually walked virtually the entire length of the Trail from Mount Katahdin in Maine to Mount Oglethorpe in Georgia." Likewise, she acclaims the merits of the A.T. movement stating, "There are now many clubs, with a total membership of over ten thousand members, actively cooperating on maintenance and use of the Trail." With those comments strengthening her case for publication of Myron's article, Jean submits not only the entire text of his arduous manuscript but also no less than seventy-two photographs! No wonder her letter concludes with reference to the considerable time and expense her preparation of these materials has taken.

Jean and Myron did not have long to wait for *National Geographic*'s verdict. In a straightforward, six-sentence letter dated November 2, 1934, Dr. Showalter and his associate, a Mr. Hildebrand, rejected Avery's article as being "too technical a paper, lacking in color, adventure, and human interest, whose appeal would be more or less weak other than to inveterate hickers [sic] and trail blazers." Mr. Hildebrand likewise agrees that Avery's article "might be condensed and popularized for such a publication as the Magazine Section of the *New York Times* or for one or another of the good out-of-doors magazines."

We can only speculate on the emotions that Jean suppressed when on November 9 she retaliated with a two-page letter that describes Avery's article as "too good to be 'wasted' on so ephemeral a publication as the *New York Times*." She goes on to snub the decision by *National Geographic*, as she details the widening appeal of the Trail project to "a large proportion of the educated people of the East" as well as a tremendously growing interest from the central and western states. Not to be defeated, she concludes by informing Dr. Showalter and Mr. Hildebrand that she had simultaneously submitted a copy of Myron's manuscript to a "well-known publisher" who suggested it be expanded into a book for which "there was an adequate market."

That series of communications with *National Geographic* demonstrates Jean's strength of character and her ambition for the success of the trail project — a strength and ambition equal to Avery's. And, while those early efforts to publish information on the Appalachian Trail in *National Geographic* did not meet with success, Jean and Myron would eventually witness the publishing of an extensive article and photographs about the Trail in it in 1949.

A handwritten note, undated but within the ATC "Stephenson Correspondence of 1934-1938" box, expressed Myron's confidence in Jean's ability to guide the trail project in a direction that would meet with his high standards, While containing very little beyond common expressions of friendliness, Myron's chosen words hinted at a mutually respectful relationship between equals.

The note began with the words, "Dear Jean," and continues, "I am pleased and satisfied [with your work].... I expect to add nothing." Their working relationship was further defined in his closing remark, "We will finish it some night next week — either Tuesday or Monday." He closed with, "Many thanks for the most interesting letter" and signed his note," Sincerely, Myron."

Apparently, Jean's work meets or exceeds his expectations, and that includes the expectation that she will join him in the office most evenings to finish what they had begun. And, so their work continues.

I was born in the South. But I was raised in New England, so when I first followed the Appalachian Trail through the Maine woods it was like returning home.

"Impressions of the Maine Wilderness," by Jean Stephenson

BUILDING THE APPALACHIAN TRAIL IN MAINE

In 1933, Myron Avery and fellow PATC members Frank Schairer and Al Jackson — accompanied by Walter Greene, a New York City actor who vacationed regularly in Maine, and Shailer Philbrick, a geologist who a few years earlier undertook a detailed topographic and geologic map of the area — carried the first terminus sign, buckets of white and blue paint, brushes, tools, and the iconic measuring wheel to Katahdin's summit in the three-year-old Baxter State Park, Maine. The often-published photograph of them passing through the boulders to the summit almost never notes that second behind Avery and his wheel is Marion Park. As Laura and Guy Waterman vividly detail in their book, *Forest and Craig*:

> *They planted their post in the summit cairn of Katahdin, nailed up a board sign, declared it the northern terminus of the A.T. and began marking with paint and cairns across the Tableland and down the Hunt Trail, heading for Georgia.... In that pioneering fortnight's work, Avery's wheel recorded 118.7 miles from the summit of Katahdin.*

Avery, familiar with the wilderness of his native state, soon established a tradition of leading summer work trips to Maine to blaze and build the Appalachian Trail in the state. Realizing that much work remained to be done to complete the trail in Maine, Avery's strategy was to infuse his small band of Washington trail workers with his love of the Maine woods in order to provide the required — although distant — work force to build and maintain it. Members of PATC and ATC, including Jean, enthusiastically joined in those annual trips to experience the Maine wilderness, a land very different from the relatively tame Virginia mountains. While those trips included hiking, canoeing, and camping, their main purpose was trail work.

The first such organized club trip occurred from August 23 to September 6, 1935. Jean was quick to sign on to this northern adventure. In a letter dated September 27, 1935, fourteen participants including Jean heartedly express their gratitude to Myron for "the splendid trip which your excellent planning and leadership made possible. In all respects that expedition was, both in conception and execution, an admirable performance. We realize that fact more and more clearly each time we indulge in the happy memories of those two weeks." Clearly, Avery had attracted just the right PATC members to accompany him on this expedition, as their words reflect both a growing love for the Maine wilderness and a readiness to join Myron on future work trips to blaze and build the A.T. through this rugged wilderness.

Recalling in 1941 her earlier introduction to the Maine wilderness, Jean wrote poetically:

> *The soft moss cushioning the rocks and spreading so thick over gnarled roots was the deep pile on which I had lain as a child.... The refreshing sunlight, so different from the burning heat further south, the cool invigorating shade, the sound of the wind ever sighing through the treetops, all seemed the sun, shadow, and sound I knew so well.... So with the familiar sun overhead, trees and plants about me, and odor of pine and fir in my nostrils, I relaxed as completely as a child who has reached once more its own bed and happily rests.*

Although she was going to those woods as an adult with her trail friends, Jean wrote about them as though she was — like Myron — born to this wilderness. Myron surely may have calculated that, in order to complete the trail in

Maine, he would need those Washington trail workers, and his planned club excursions beginning in 1935 produced the desired results.

Also aware of the need to establish a trail-maintaining club in Maine to keep the Trail open, Avery founded the Maine Appalachian Trail Club in June 1935. As to be expected, many of its charter members lived and worked in far-off Washington. Club treasurer was Mary Jo Kempt; secretary was Frank Schairer. Avery served on the executive committee, while Walter Greene served as the club's first president. This arrangement, although challenging, had its benefits for Jean and her fellow hiking friends, as they now had ample reason to escape the nation's capital during the heat of summer to experience Maine's picturesque mountains and lakes.

Jean was presented with just such an opportunity in 1939, when the ATC chose Daicey Pond below Katahdin as the site for its ninth general meeting. She did not balk at undertaking the job of organizing this event despite the obvious challenges. Her first job was to secure lodging for those expected to attend the event, a task that was complicated by the difficulties of communicating with the owners of sporting camps. Her letters inquiring about number and type of sleeping accommodations, dining options, train schedules, and shuttle services by truck and canoe to local trails often took weeks to stir a response from backwoods camp owners. Jean faced these challenges with patience, courtesy, and efficiency. Perhaps she could not change the slow pace of life in the Maine woods, but, from ATC and PATC's Washington office, Jean was spurred into action. A budget for the event, a daily schedule of activities, and a reservation system were soon set up.

As the weeks and months passed, Jean's letter-writing began to produce responses from the camp owners with the information that she needed, such as the number of available beds, dining hall capacities, and local train schedules, as well as arrangements for canoe trips, hikes, and plane rides into remote areas. Jean's letters were full of every detail, down to her labeling bed assignments for the expected sixty participants.

PATC was well represented at the general meeting, with twenty-seven members even staying on for an additional week of exploring in the Katahdin area and another week of hiking the A.T. in Maine. The success of the meeting and the extended stay was expressed in Dorothy Swift's report in PATC's *Bulletin*. Here she describes the "beautiful scenery, good weather, a full moon on

Ambejijus Lake, comfortable camps, wild blueberries, and little alpine flowers." Such pleasant memories lingered, but briefly.

Upon their return to the nation's capital, Jean and her fellow hiking friends became increasing aware of the escalating conflicts in Europe. Those dramatic global events contrasted sharply with their experiences of Maine's balsam forests, glassy lakes, and star-filled night skies. The contrast would only sharpen Jean's memories of the Maine woods and strengthen her determination to return. Changes were coming as the United States watched Britain and France enter the war against Germany and the Soviet Union invade Poland.

Those events of international importance were also soon to alter the working relationship that Jean was beginning to enjoy with Myron Avery.

I have secured, informally, the views of various persons, from various sections of the country, who are interested in the Trail project. I believe I am now in a position to make definite recommendations. If these recommendations are approved by the Board of Managers, I can form a committee and proceed to carry them into effect.

Jean Stephenson letter to Myron Avery, January 3, 1938

A RELATIONSHIP THAT WORKS

Indications that Myron had confidence in Jean's abilities can be found as early as June 1937, when she was appointed chairman of ATC's membership committee. When the board of managers asked her to investigate ways and means of increasing membership in the Conference as a way of increasing revenues, Jean set to work developing new membership application procedures and membership categories. Up until this time, the Conference offered just three classes of membership: Class A and B for organizations that maintained sections of the Trail or gave financial assistance for maintenance of the Trail, and Class C for certain public officials who supervised sections of the Trail.

In a written report to Myron on January 3, 1938, Jean outlined her idea for a separate class of membership for individuals. Her plan was to gain additional financial support for the ATC by drawing into membership those individuals not affiliated with a local hiking club who wished to support the Appalachian Trail project. Her goal was to bring in dues from this previously untapped reservoir of outdoor enthusiasts.

Jean's report earned Myron's immediate approval, and he presented it to the board, asking that her membership program become effective after a ten-day review period. When board member Paul Fink suggested that all invitations to membership be signed by Myron Avery, as board chairman, for reasons of "psychology," Myron objected. Flatly denying any need for his signature on membership letters, Myron stated that Jean would be entrusted with writing the membership acceptance letters and signing them with her own name.

In delegating that responsibility to Jean, he openly acknowledged both her capabilities and his belief that she would get the job done without his oversight. Jean was one A.T. worker that he did not have to prod in order to get the results he desired and, quite often, demanded from others involved in the Trail project. Perhaps Myron had begun to recognize that Jean possessed a driving ambition equal to his own.

In 1939, Jean took on a flurry of activities in the local Potomac club and in the national conference. Several were of limited duration, and others would consume her for decades. When her position with the U.S. Navy Bureau of Supplies and Accounts was expanded to include editorial work in its publications division, Jean was poised to bring her work-related skills to the ATC as well.

Thus she volunteered in 1939 to prepare and pay for the first two issues of an ATC newsletter, to be called the *Appalachian Trailway News*. Her work on various committees up until that time convinced Jean of the need to communicate information about the Trail to both those working within the Trail community and the general public. She reasoned that, without a regularly published newsletter, how could the Appalachian Trail project become sustainable? As might be expected, those first issues, published in 1939, met with immediate success.

However, when three other Trail volunteers were asked to continue the project, they declined. Emphasizing her conviction that the ATC *needed* a regularly published newsletter, Jean took on the task. At this time, she could not know that she would leave her greatest visible legacy to the Trail project in this role as the ATC's newsletter editor.

As 1939 drew to a close, Jean was able to report to Myron, "While there is still much to be done to acquaint the public with the pleasures of woods walking, the Trail, and the aids to its use in the way of guides and maps…., much has been accomplished this year." As chair of PATC's publicity committee, Jean presents the accomplishments of her committee in the *Report of the Eleventh Annual Meeting of the Potomac Appalachian Trail Club.* They include getting notices of every PATC trip in at least one Washington paper, securing club publicity in government departments that resulted in government workers participating in forty-two walks with total attendance of 1,056, placing Trail stories in newspapers of towns adjacent to the Trail, and publishing a twenty-four page booklet on how to prepare Trail news releases.

Jean's report reflected her growing ambitions to gain publicity for the Trail project, to recruit government workers to the club, and to provide current members with guidance on how they also could assist with publicizing the Trail project and bringing new recruits to the effort. The accomplishments of her committee clearly indicate that Jean had taken on a variety of responsibilities, carried out the duties, and produced significant results. Jean was becoming a major contributor to the success of the Appalachian Trail project in those early years.

Evidenced there also is the evolving relationship between Myron and Jean, two exceptionally well-educated people who shared a powerful commitment to advance the Appalachian Trail project. Further evidenced is Jean's growing determination to work beside him — and not necessarily behind him — to build this long-distance trail and the organization to sustain it. Within Jean's report of 1939 was a portrayal of a woman capable of matching Myron's fiery spirit. As the report was presented to the Potomac club, Myron and the entire club leadership were clearly made aware of the passion that Jean possessed for the Trail project — a passion that would last her lifetime.

When Myron's prewar work as an admiralty lawyer in the U.S. Maritime Commission required that he move to New York early in 1940, he submitted his resignation to PATC in June. Jean was among those members who spoke out against the PATC's accepting the resignation. Myron bowed to their wishes only to retender his resignation again in November, this time in anger. Even though he was managing the club from afar as best he could, Avery learned that the council had approved a schedule of activities for the club's climbing

Jean, right, in a portrait accompanying an article in a sorority magazine, and below in sun hat, on an early hike.

Jean (left) with others outside the Washington headquarters of ATC/PATC.

Jean is seated at center (dark cap) on a PATC blazing trip with Myron Avery (sunglasses). Middle photograph: Jean (center) at Chairback Gap in Maine, taken by Sadie Giller. To its right, the front of the inaugural issue of the Appalachian Trailway News *in January 1939. Below is Jean's packing list for the 1939 meeting (left) and (right) 1935 postcards to Avery from Jean and Marion Park on hiking trips.*

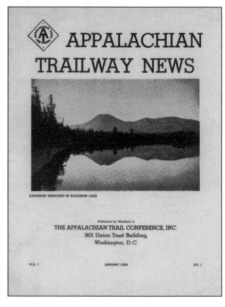

Top: Jean, with bandanna, on Sentinel Mountain in 1939 with Myron Avery (left), Earl York, Jr., and Kathryn Fulkerson during the ninth general meeting, based at the Yorks' Twin Pines Camps (right). Above, discovered among Jean's private photograph collection was this snapshot of Avery playfully objecting to his portrait.

Above left, true Jean either composing poetry on the Trail or making notes for a guidebook or article. Above right, with Sadye Giller (left), heading out for a day of painting blazes along the new Trail in Maine in the mid-1930s. Middle, on a hike in 1950 with Sadye (right) and a group from the Natural Bridge A.T. Club. At right, the most-published, classic photograph of Jean Stephenson as editor and stalwart office volunteer, taking care of ATC and PATC business.

Clockwise from right: Jean on the Trail (undated); on the 1935 PATC/MATC trip to place a new Katahdin summit sign, Avery is at left and Marion Park and Jean are to his immediate left; at a meeting in 1971 with NPS land-acquisition chief Richard Stanton; one of Jean's genealogy texts; and leaving a new shelter in Maine.

group — activities that he strongly felt interfered with the club's true purposes of hiking, trail-building, and trail maintenance. His resignation was now an expression of his disapproval of those auxiliary club activities, as well as a fateful acceptance that management of the club from a distance was falling short of the high standards that he set for himself and the Potomac club. This time, Jean wrote an emotionally charged letter to Myron imploring him to reconsider, with the result that he again withdrew his resignation.

However, his message to the club membership was clear: He would officially step down as the PATC president at the club's thirteenth annual meeting scheduled for January 28, 1941.

Jean's working relationship with Myron would extend for another eleven years, as he continued as chairman of the ATC. The Potomac club, however, would have to seek a new president. The club's council minutes of June 1940 honored his many years of leadership by stating, "Myron could never be replaced, even though his office might be filled."

As Myron began his second decade as chairman of ATC, Jean willingly expanded her office duties into other areas of Trail management. Those included editing and publishing the *Appalachian Trailway News* and an assortment of guidebooks, organizing the ATC's meetings, maintaining liaison to federal and state officials, providing materials to ATC's board of managers, and corresponding with Trail maintaining clubs all along the East Coast.

Just as Myron's early prodding of his Trail-builders from Maine to Georgia resulted in the 1937 initial completion of Appalachian Trail, Jean now took over prodding each maintaining club to report trail conditions, relocations, and improvements to her on a regular basis. Her letters reached up and down the length of the Trail, requesting timely reports, which were then edited and placed with regularity in the newsletter. With Jean as editor, the *Appalachian Trailway News* offered a complete report of Trail news, and those Conference members who regularly received the newsletter were reminded constantly of the importance of volunteer maintainers to the success of the Trail project.

The early issues of the *Appalachian Trailway News* were designed to meet Jean's original goal of the newsletter: to knit together the maintaining clubs and the membership at all levels in a common goal to build, maintain, and protect the Appalachian Trail.

Jean also became increasing active in the Maine Appalachian Trail Club, of which she was a charter member. As publicity committee chair for the Maine club, Jean led a reinvigorated campaign in the early 1940s to publicize the Trail in Maine. She boasted in a club newsletter, "The Trail is in usable condition throughout Maine, and we have revitalized the Maine Appalachian Trail Club."

Assisted by the ATC's slides custodian, Mrs. Donald Jacobs, Jean organized the shipping of a slide show to a variety of Maine organizations. In addition, she prepared a 3,000-word article for *The Rangeley Record*, 10,000 copies of which were given away at Maine sportsman shows. An additional 30,000 copies were sent to every state for distribution at similar shows. Color posters also were distributed to Maine businesses and camps. When the Maine trail maintainers planned an informal meeting, Jean arranged a personal trip to be in the area, and, with Avery's consent, she attended the meeting.

I leave you with your Task — your Pleasure — the Heritage of the Trail Club — that long brown path from Katahdin…to be held open and intact until the return of better days.

Myron Avery speech, "The Heritage of the Potomac Appalachian Trail Club," November 20, 1941

THE WAR YEARS

Benton MacKaye had envisioned in his 1921 article that the Trail would serve as respite for busy factory laborers, city dwellers in the East Coast metropolis, and those in mental distress. That would hold true for members of the Appalachian Trail Conference and its early maintaining clubs as the United States entered World War II. The early 1940s was a time of many uncertainties and anxieties, for which the Trail could offer at least a temporary escape for hikers and maintainers.

By early 1942, the war the United States had just entered fully after Pearl Harbor in December 1941 was having a noticeable effect on the Appalachian Trail Conference, its maintaining clubs, and the Trail itself. Some effects were material-based. Gasoline and tires were strictly rationed, and, consequently, many club records noted difficulties with finding transportation to get work parties to the Trail to perform routine maintenance. Additionally, many Trail overseers were called into the armed services, leaving sections of the Trail without the needed leadership to organize work trips or the required skills to complete maintenance tasks. For example, the Potomac club suffered the loss of Frank Schairer, when he stepped down in January 1943 after twelve years as supervisor of overseers. The celebrated geochemist was now "engaged in war work" that took him away from the city several days each week, returning too late on Sundays to join in the club's work trips. Despite the challenges brought on by the war, the Potomac club reported in the autumn of 1942 that a planned chain of lean-tos from the Susquehanna River in Pennsylvania to Rockfish Gap in Virginia was completed — a total of thirty-five shelters. Not surprisingly, Myron Avery was behind this effort. Despite resigning as president of the Potomac club in January of the previous year, being called into active duty in 1942, and relocating to New York, Avery had nevertheless remained in charge of PATC's shelter-building program. Prodding club members from so great a distance to accelerate their efforts and complete shelters at Ashby Gap, Keys Gap, and three other locations in northern Virginia proved frustrating and irritating almost beyond what Avery could bear. As noted in Bates' *Breaking Trail in the Central Appalachians,* Avery's frustrations spewed out in his letters from New York to the Potomac club shelters committee members. In his May 29, 1941, letter to John Burlew, now serving as chairman of the shelters committee, Avery writes, "The whole lean-to business has been a source of disappointment to me in its failure to reach completion and the staggering increase in expense." But, in the end, his efforts prevailed, and the shelter chain was completed — a remarkable accomplishment during an extraordinary time.

Following the example of women all across the country, who stepped in to fill many jobs held previously by men now serving in the armed services, women in the Trail clubs stepped up to help maintain the Trail. In his January 1943 report to the Potomac club, Schairer noted, "Now slightly over 25 percent of our overseers are serving with the armed forces of the country." He also reports, "Under present conditions, about 65 percent of the crew are women; while they may not have as much physical strength, they seem able to accomplish the work."

As recalled by Florence Nichol, a longtime volunteer for the Appalachian Trail Conference and the Potomac A.T. Club, "The theory was that, when our soldiers got home from the war, they would have this form of recreation. It was our patriotic duty to keep the Trail open."

While restrictions on gas and tires and reductions in the number of male trail maintainers greatly challenged clubs up and down the East Coast to keep their respective sections of the A.T. open, the war did not diminish the spirit of the Trail project. An ATC vice chairman and president of the Mountain Club of Maryland, O.O. Heard, was quoted in the September 1942 issue of the *Appalachian Trailway News* as declaring, "Plan by all means to work your assigned section of The Appalachian Trail come hell or high water, for there will be need of its recreational value when Victory comes." For many of these volunteer maintainers, their trail work helped to counterbalance the difficulties and uncertainties brought on by a country at war.

As recalled by Florence Nichol, Jean Stephenson organized many of the work trips during those war years. Jean, who was now serving officially as secretary of PATC's overseers committee, set up a program to ensure that work trips continued on a regular basis. She maintained a list of prospective trail workers and, as a name came up on the list, that worker would be invited to attend the next scheduled work trip. Failure to attend would place the worker at the end of the list. Aware of this rotation and not wanting to be passed over, Florence admitted that she went on nearly every trip for a long time. Beginning in January 1943, a "wartime program" also became part of the club's monthly calendar, with only one work trip being held in the first half of the month and one hike in the second part of the month. Because of the restrictions on private car transportation, the club limited work trips to thirty participants and began using a truck, its bed filled with straw. Trail workers responded with high spirits, as Florence stated, "By the time you got to the Trail, you really didn't know what legs were yours." Trail women such as Florence and Jean stepped up to fill the void in the ranks of the Trail maintainers to ensure that, to the best of their abilities, the Trail remained open.

Nevertheless, scant resources and absent Trail workers were the realities of the war years. As a result, maintenance was curtailed and some sections of the Trail became overgrown, blazing became indistinguishable, signs deteriorated or disappeared, and shelters occasionally were vandalized. Assistance sometimes was found in unlikely places, such as when occupants of two conscientious-objector camps in Shenandoah National Park were sent out to reclear an overgrown section of the Trail in the park. Those nontraditional Trail workers joined forces with the women club members to answer the call to "active Trail duty."

Beyond material sacrifices such as gas rationing and mental anxieties for those serving in the war effort, club members experienced another type of hardship brought on by the war — a loss of Trail camaraderie.

The same restrictions that limited work trips also caused clubs to hold fewer business meetings. Social events became rare, hiking trips were limited to nearby destinations, and overnight and week-long excursions to distant sections of the Trail were curtailed. For Jean and many other club members, limiting their times together and their times on the Trail created a real emptiness in their lives.

As editor of ATC's *Appalachian Trailway News*, Jean regularly reported on those club members who were called into active duty. The Potomac club also made accommodations to forego the annual dues for service men and women, ensuring that their membership would remain active and their welcome home would include an open invitation to return to Trail work.

Club newsletters and correspondences unfailingly expressed optimism that the current hardships were but temporary. The tone of writing remained upbeat, as though the very existence of the Trail — regardless of its condition, the infrequency of work trips, and the missing of good times with Trail friends — provided them with solace.

Those war years would pass, and the Trail would be waiting. It was just a matter of time...and patience.

Reason oft given to join the Trail Club
Is communion with nature, the mountains, the sky —
But unannounced bonus may come with a hike,
A new kindred spirit you very much like
And travel with 'til you die."

Anonymous, from PATC Bulletin, November 1977

TRAIL FRIENDSHIPS

Jean Stephenson never married. In fact, no PATC or ATC records indi-cate she was ever interested in romance. This is worth noting, since A.T. clubs offered ample opportunity for socializing that often led to match-making. Both single and married members enjoyed activities such as square dancing, banquets, talent shows, and overnight excursions in addition to day hiking. Trail clubs brought people of similar interests together, sometimes under harsh weather, primitive accommodations, and hard physical work. Such conditions certainly offered insight into the character of fellow hikers, and, for those club members who were well-suited for the outdoor life, those hardships translated into "jolly good times." If there were mutual interest, Trail happiness could lead to Trail romance.

Marriages among club members occurred with regularity. PATC's early records indicate a marriage between club members in 1931 and another 1935, two in 1936, one in 1938, and three in 1939. PATC member Dorothy Kemball Walker documented many of those Trail marriages in her article, "Kindred Spirits." Dorothy conducted a survey of club members and interviewed those who actually met through PATC activities and then married. Her findings begin with Harold "Andy" Anderson and Edna Thomas who met in 1933 on a club hike to the top of Mary's Rock and extended to John (Jack) Hess and Amanda Leek, who met in 1944 while enduring a ride in the back of the club's truck, the Red Beauty, on an apple-picking trip. Several couples even reported honeymooning at PATC shelters, most likely keeping their exact location a secret from their prankster-loving club friends!

Although apparently not leading to romance, Jean's memberships in PATC, ATC, and MATC provided her with something she was seeking — lasting friendship. In the late 1940s and early 1950s, the energetic and feisty Sadye Giller was one of Jean's special Trail friends.

Together, those two women shared many adventures in the Maine woods, as well as similar careers in the Department of the Navy and interests in the study of genealogy. Sadye joined PATC in 1946 and ATC two years later. In 1948 and 1949, Sadye accompanied Jean on her summer forays to the Maine woods. They were true adventurers as they painted the standard white A.T.

blaze on trees along more than twenty miles of the Appalachian Trail, traveling between sports camps on foot, by canoe, and occasionally by plane. (See photograph on page 46.) As usual, Jean handled the advance arrangements through a string of correspondence to camp owners, pilots, and other local contacts established by her and Avery's past Trail work in Maine.

Sadye provided the spirited companionship, boundless energy, and fearless sense of adventure that Jean enjoyed in her Trail companions. Jean and Sayde humorously declared themselves the only members of the "Ladies Auxiliary of the Maine A.T. Club," but many who knew of their work on the Trail in Maine recognized them as accomplished Trail maintainers. For both women, their days on the Trail in Maine were filled with the joy of being in the North Woods and of being Trail friends.

Also, for both women, the love for the Trail and its special lands translated into a lifelong dedication to the Trail project. Sadye served as volunteer treasurer of ATC for a remarkable twenty-two years, spending every Saturday afternoon at the ATC headquarters completing financial records — except for those times when she and Jean were drawn to Maine's woods for two weeks of spirited Trail work.

Likewise, for the twenty-five years that she served as editor of the *Appalachian Trailway News*, Jean scheduled all of her trips and other personal obligations around the newsletter's editing and publishing schedule. Sadye and Jean became kindred spirits in all things Trail-related.

Enclosed is the writeup you requested. If it fails to cover the subject thoroughly enough or is otherwise unsuitable, please outline for me what should be done and I will be glad to work on it some more.

Earl Shaffer, in a 1948 letter to Jean Stephenson

A LONG, LONELY TREK

Word had been traveling up and down the Appalachian Trail for weeks. A lone hiker from York, Pennsylvania, had set out to walk the entire 2,000 miles-plus from Mount Oglethorpe in Georgia to Katahdin in Maine in one continuous hike. To many in the Appalachian Trail clubs, such a hike was unthinkable. Could it be done? Why would it be done? What type of person would set out to do it?

As word traveled back to the Appalachian Trail Conference, Jean Stephenson and Myron Avery were among those who expressed skepticism. Their doubts were not reflective of what Earl Shaffer had set out to do or of the merits of such an accomplishment. Rather Jean and Myron shared the notion that the purpose of the Trail was for "woods walking" as a leisure activity, not as a singular, epic journey. Nevertheless, National Park Service rangers, forest fire wardens, local reporters, and numerous town folk along the A.T. route were substantiating the report that Earl Shaffer had indeed followed the long, brown path through their consecutive areas on a journey of extraordinary and perhaps unimaginable proportions. And so, Jean set about collecting the details directly from the most reliable source — Earl Shaffer.

Writing in response to Jean's request for information about his long journey, Earl acknowledged her suggestion that he meet with Avery. Earl offered to meet with Avery in Washington just prior to Earl's "coming back up to Baltimore for a showing the following day (Dec 2)." Earl ended his letter with a request to Jean, "I wish you would let me know if he [Myron Avery] is expecting me to write," and he enclosed an essay that documented his achievement, titled "The Long Cruise."

In this seven-page essay, Earl outlines the motivations and preparations for his hike; his equipment, preferred foods, daily routine, and clothing; and the challenges of weather, snake bite, and traveling alone. The information that Earl offered was convincing; he presented himself as exceptionally capable of such a feat. He also expressed a genuine love of wilderness travel and described himself as "robust enough to withstand considerable rigor," having avoided the use of tobacco and alcoholic drinks. He then closed "The Long Cruise" with a poignant response to the question, "Why would someone set out to hike the entire A.T. as one continuous journey?" Earl stated, "Before the war there were two of us…." He described fellow soldier Walter Winemiller as "a partner such as one may have only once in life." But, as the war came to a close, Earl returned from Iwo Jima alone, carrying with him a dream that they had once shared — to hike the Appalachian Trail. He ended his essay with the words, "No incentive could have been stronger to carry me over the long high Trail than remembering we always wanted to hike it together."

In that letter exchange, Jean found the information she needed to speak to Myron, to arrange for them to meet, and to substantiate Earl's claim of completing the first thru-hike of the Appalachian Trail. An "unthinkable" accomplishment was indeed achieved. Shaffer said decades later that the meeting with Avery never occurred, although he did travel at least once to meet with Benton MacKaye.

The A.T. groups have lost a great leader and those who knew him, a friend who can never be replaced.

Appalachian Trailway News, September 1952

THE LOSS OF MYRON AVERY

The 1952 general meeting of the Appalachian Trail Conference was held at Skyland, Virginia, in Shenandoah National Park from May 30 to June 1 and was hosted by the Potomac Appalachian Trail Club. Since Avery had resigned as chairman at the beginning of the year, ATC's Vice Chairman Murray H. Stevens presided over the meeting, noting in his opening remarks that Myron had found it necessary, because of continued illness, to cancel on the previous day his plans to attend. Jean and her many Trail friends enjoyed the familiarity and relative simplicity of organizing the event on the Potomac club's home territory. Jean described the event as "an exceptionally good one." Always seeking news articles to include in upcoming issues of the *Appalachian Trailway News,* she wrote to a Mr. Sieker on July 25, 1952, requesting he proofread her transcription of a talk he gave at the meeting. In the letter, she expressed one of her few regrets about the event: Myron Avery was not in attendance.

Acting on the advice of medical specialists in New York in January, Avery had resigned from the Navy, stepped down as chairman of ATC, and at the last minute decided not to attend the ATC general meeting. Instead, he and his family went to his hometown of Lubec, Maine, in June. It was a trip meant to refresh and restore an exhausted, over-worked, and repeatedly (secretly) hospitalized man. Jean's letter to Mr. Sieker concluded, "You will be glad to hear that Myron is at his home in Lubec, Maine, and will return here in September,

I believe. He seems to be getting along very well, and I look to see him on the Trail with us next year."

That was not to be. The next day — July 26, 1952 — while on a 10-day excursion to Nova Scotia with his younger son, Hal, Avery suffered a massive heart attack on the grounds of Fort Anne National Historical Park and died instantly. Jean officially recorded his death in the *Report of the Twelfth Appalachian Trail Conference*, but, in a letter written the day after Avery's death to Roy Fairfield of Biddeford, Maine, we gain insight into her sense of personal loss. Jean writes:

> *Myron was one of the finest men I have ever known and I can hardly realize how it will be to be without him. He was so much like my father and younger brother who died years ago that he had gradually come to take their place in my life…. From the personal side, his place can never be filled.*

Jean's expression of loss is touching; however, it contrasted sharply with the balance of her letter. She goes on to outline her upcoming travel plans to Maine, during which time she can arrange for a meeting with Maine A.T. Club officers to decide about electing a new president. She closes with a postscript telling about a professor in Maine who has a group that wants to maintain a section of the A.T. and outlining how to identify what section of the Trail may be best to assign to the group. The apparent ease with which Jean transitions from tender reflections of Myron to A.T. business is not necessarily reflective of a lack of sincerity, but rather demonstrates the depth of her commitment to the Appalachian Trail project. It's the trait that she shared with Myron Avery and many of the early Trail builders. Their personal relationships and their contributions to the Trail had a beginning and an end; the Appalachian Trail would endure.

With Myron's death, a long partnership ended. Perhaps their mutual love for the Maine woods made returning to Maine especially poignant for Jean. In July 1968, she wrote a letter to Maine A.T. Club President Dave Field, thanking him for assistance in editing sections of the *Maine Appalachian Trail Guide*, and adding, "It occurred to me that you and Myron Avery would have worked well together!" She continued, "Sometimes even now, when I go over a section I had never been on before, but have read his description, it seems as if I am merely revisiting it, for it seems so familiar." Sixteen years had passed since

Myron's death, and yet Jean so vividly recalled those times when — with Myron writing and Jean editing — she was transported to a seemingly familiar, though unvisited, part of the great North Woods.

Without Jean in her key position, we'd all be floundering around.

Gannon Coffey, President of the Georgia Appalachian Trail Club,
August 1963

TRAVELING MAINE TO TEXAS

Looking across the broad spectrum of Jean's service to ATC, Myron's death was indeed an unexpected and tragic event; however, she continued on with her Trail work. For example, with the same consistency of effort, Jean continued as editor of the *Appalachian Trailway News*, where for two-and-a-half decades she would be the voice of (and to) maintaining clubs, volunteers, and the general public as the Trail project grew to national status. Jean also continued to enjoy hiking in Maine.

In June 1955, she wrote an article, "Camping at Katahdin," for the Appalachian Mountain Club's magazine, *Appalachia*. With her nephew and two of his young friends as companions, Jean organized a trip to Katahdin, and she served as guide for their twelve-day backpacking trip through Baxter State Park. Having hiked together in the close-to-home Southern Appalachians, that trip was Jean's first opportunity to introduce those young hikers to her beloved Maine. At age sixty-three, Jean showed no signs of slowing down as she led them — with men carrying thirty-five-pound packs and women thirty-pound packs — to a series of backcountry campgrounds that required wading across the south branch of the Wassataquoik River and maneuvering the Knife Edge to summit Katahdin. Jean was not slowing down. However, changes were on the horizon for the A.T. project that would test her ability to adapt and endure.

In 1961, the possibility of the destruction of much of the A.T. in Georgia by a proposed Blue Ridge Parkway extension cast a cloud over members of the Georgia Appalachian Trail Club (GATC). Although the threat would languish for many years, the Georgia club received consistent support from ATC and many within the Trail community. Gannon Coffey, then president of the Georgia club, went so far as to write to Benton MacKaye and offer an all expenses-paid invitation for him to attend their club's annual meeting with the hopes of inspiring members to "fight this vast bureaucracy and never-ending desire to satisfy the motorist." While Benton was unable to come, Jean, in her strategic position in ATC's Washington headquarters, went into action by becoming "coordinator of the Blue Ridge matter." In her usually thorough fashion, Jean began by studying topographical maps to make herself familiar with the Georgia mountain areas, the current route of the A.T., and the possibilities of acceptable alternatives for both the Trail and the proposed parkway. She then began her campaign by meeting with parkway officials and engineers and "making it clear to all concerned that the position of the Appalachian Trail Conference was that we did not want interference with the Trail in Georgia... and that our local members were willing to help work out a route that would be acceptable to the traveling public and yet would not interfere with the Trail."

Early in 1963, sensing that the parkway issue would not be settled quickly and would increasingly take up more of Jean's time than ATC was willing to offer, Stanley Murray, chairman of ATC's board of managers, stepped up his involvement. He began by visiting Georgia in July and then continuing to press for a favorable resolution. As we would expect, Jean continued her work in Washington, and Coffey later wrote to Murray, "It goes without saying that without Jean in her key position, we'd all be floundering around. The ten feet of topographic map she sent just before your visit here was a production which convinced me of the professional character of her office and the variety of skills required." Once again, Jean worked on. In Georgia, as elsewhere along the full length of the A.T., Jean demonstrated first her abilities, second her perseverance, and lastly her unmatched devotion to the Trail. Nevertheless, the threat of an extension of the Blue Ridge Parkway would continue to plague the Georgia club and ATC until a university woman named Margaret Drummond came to the presidency of GATC and carried the "torch" that Jean lit. Only then would the parkway issue fade into obscurity at last. (See Chapter 5.)

Jean's influences also extended to the other end of the Appalachian Trail. Here, the Maine A.T. Club was finally prepared in February 1967 to offer twenty-four private landowners, mostly timber companies, a memorandum of agreement (MOA) establishing, at a minimum, a one-quarter mile zone on each side of the Trail in which development inconsistent with the Trail corridor would be prohibited. Although the document's wording was clear in prohibiting new motorized roads paralleling the Trail corridor, it became somewhat lengthy and vague regarding logging activities near the corridor. Jean led the Trail community's expectations that the agreements, once signed by landowners, would provide an acceptable level of protection of the A.T. corridor from clear-cut logging. As with the Georgia parkway issue, this was an issue near and dear to Jean and one in which she was prepared to commit her time and experience into winning.

Although by mid-March it had become apparent that most landowners were balking at signing such an agreement, Jean showed no hesitation in writing to perhaps the largest and most formidable landowner, Great Northern Paper Company. Great Northern had earlier expressed its objections to the agreement in letters to both its Maine senator and MATC's president. Nevertheless, Jean headed straight into the controversy.

With a quiet but firm confidence, Jean wrote to John T. Maines of Great Northern Paper Company warning that, in the absence of signing the proposed agreement, landowners such as Great Northern may find themselves in a less favorable position when the federal government enacted the pending national trails system bill. Her letter — four pages in length, more than 1,400 words, and true to Jean's typical thoroughness — avoided direct controversy, instead citing areas in which the company and the Trail project were seeking mutually beneficial results. However, her repeated reference to pending federal action served as a warning to the paper company to accept the terms of the memorandum or face harsher terms mandated by enactment of the bill.

Jean knew exactly where the strengths of the Trail project lay in this battle for corridor protection, and she played to those strengths. Her formidable closing to this letter included these words, "I hope you will feel you can and may be able to convince your colleagues that the agreements we have suggested should be signed now, not only as a matter of 'good public relations' but also as 'good business.'"

By April 22, and surely as a direct result of Jean's letter to Maines, James Faulkner, president of the Maine Appalachian Trail Club, reported that Great Northern Paper Company had signed the MOA. He aptly used this accomplishment to leverage other landowners, such as the International Paper Company, to also sign. Jean had clearly matured as a Trail negotiator and was now

considered the preferred mediator to have on the Trail side of landowner negotiations. Sitting opposite her at the negotiating table proved to be a challenge,
even for executives such as those of Great Northern Paper.

Also in the 1960s, Jean also renewed her interest in genealogy, but, where
earlier she was drawn by an amateur interest in the history of the mountain
families of the Shenandoah region, now she approached the subject with a
scholarly passion.

In a letter dated June 9, 1966, to the Shenandoah Publishing House, providing her edits to an ATC publication soon to be reprinted, Jean wrote in a
postscript that she was leaving for Birmingham, Alabama, "to handle the Genealogical Institute of Samford University." Again, in a letter dated November
23, 1967, seeking editorial assistance in the writing of the *Katahdin Guide,*
Jean made reference to an upcoming trip to Ft. Worth, Texas, where she was
to speak to the Texas State Genealogical Society. The same letter contained
reference to trips to Richmond, Virginia; Sante Fe, New Mexico; Charleston,
South Carolina; and Columbia, Maryland. Her retirement from the U.S. Navy
in 1950 allowed her the time for traveling to speak at genealogical conferences,
just as it afforded her the time to backpack with her nephew and other friends.

The National Genealogical Society described Jean as "a pioneer genealogical educator." She balanced her work in this field with her many commitments
to the Appalachian Trail, and she even managed to take on more responsibilities and assume more roles. For example, Jean served as secretary of the American Society of Genealogists; councilor, chairman of publications, and editor of
the National Genealogical Society's *Quarterly;* cofounder and president of the
Board of Certification of Genealogists; codirector of the National Institute on
Genealogical Research; and founding instructor of Samford University's Institute of Genealogy & Historical Research. Jean was also well-published in this
area, having authored or coauthored such works as *Heraldry for the American
Genealogist* and *Scotch-Irish Migration to South Carolina,* which are consulted
to this day. Those accomplishments, which eventually led to her posthumous
election to the National Genealogical Hall of Fame, recognize Jean as a respected scholar and author — talents that she perfected through her government career and her volunteer positions within the Appalachian Trail movement.

One intense human need, an instinct as deep as for life itself, is that to do something for others and to keep alive something to be handed on to future generations.... It is this quality in the Appalachian Trail that has attracted workers to it.

"The Appalachian Trail — What is it?" by Jean Stephenson

SERVICE IS GIVEN UNSELFISHLY

Jean was not one to accept recognition for her service to the A.T. project gracefully. In fact, at the 1967 ATC general meeting, when Chairman Stan Murray informed her that honorary membership, the organization's highest recognition, would be conferred on her the next day, Jean balked. Finally, at her insistence, her name was dropped from the list of those nominated that year. At a 1972 ATC meeting, the Conference would try again to place Jean on its honorary membership rolls. At the time, Jean was preoccupied with supervising a genealogy conference in Virginia and then lecturing at another conference in Salt Lake City and, therefore, she was not present at the meeting. In her absence, she was awarded ATC's honorary membership. While she would later lecture Stan Murray on her position regarding such recognitions, Jean accepted the honorary membership at last.

The 1970s produced several dramatic changes in the management of the A.T. and, in particular, the Maine A.T. Club. With Jean approaching her eightieth birthday, change did not come easy to her. In letters, she referred to a childhood bout of pneumonia that now seemed to cause her difficulties and a recent heart ailment that limited her activities.

In February 1973, Jean found it necessary to move from her longtime apartment at the Conrad — an experience that she recounted in great detail in a letter dated April 30, 1973, to Sam Butcher, Dana Little, and Maxine Newhall of the Maine A.T. Club. The prospects of packing and moving her personal belongings did not seem to faze Jean; however, the challenges of relocating her extensive library unnerved and nearly overwhelmed her. When a tottering pile of four thousand books, forty-one full-sized metal file drawers, forty large cardboard cases, and more than one hundred cartons of papers were deposited on the sidewalks in front of Washington's Annapolis Hotel, traffic slowed to a near halt, and pedestrians searched for a safe detour. All the while, two men jostled the contents of their moving van through the hotel's open doors, into the lobby, and eventually to the waiting elevators. At age eighty, Jean did her best to direct the scene and bring order to a growing disorderly situation. Those books, boxes and files — temporarily strewn across the sidewalk — contained her life's service to the Appalachian Trail. Their relocation needed to be carefully orchestrated.

Forced from her apartment home of forty-six years to make way for a new subway station, Jean was anxious to complete this emotionally and physically taxing move. Her stork-like features, over-sized glasses, and 1950s-style knot of gray hair accentuated an expression of concern and impatience to see this valuable cargo safely deposited inside her new apartment. In the midst of this small group of onlookers, and, under Jean's watchful eye, a man suddenly leaped from a stopped car, seized a box, and sped off as the traffic light conveniently turned green. A state of utter confusion followed. Within fifteen minutes, a police officer arrived and fifty boxes similar to the one stolen were opened and their contents examined to determine what was missing. The driver of a nearby car provided the license number of the vehicle, which was quickly determined to be stolen. It would be found later, empty and abandoned.

Not to be deterred, Jean quickly identified the missing box as containing the bank statements, checkbook, and vouchers of the Maine club. Over the next several months, as the files were transferred safely into the familiar floor-to-ceiling bookcases that had always lined every wall of her living room, Jean began to gain control of the situation. Promising the newly elected treasurer to "summarize the receipts and expenditures and make up a report covering the year as nearly as I can identify things," Jean systematically outlined in her letter to club officers the actions needed to resolve several items of club business. Although she admitted that her "state of confusion" continued to linger, Jean nevertheless traveled to Maine for a meeting of the Maine club's board of directors later in 1973.

Having functioned for many years under the leadership of Myron Avery and other Washington-based Trail people, the Maine club now had local leaders serving on its board of directors. The club was ready to assert its autonomy in managing the Maine section of the A.T. Although Jean was welcome at this meeting, she was now an outsider with regard to its governance. Having recently stepped down as the club's treasurer, Jean was attending the meeting to finalize the details for publishing the latest edition of the *Maine Guide to the Appalachian Trail*.

When discussions turned to setting the retail purchase price for the guide, Jean was suddenly overcome with emotions and unable to fight back her tears. Several of those in attendance attributed her behavior to health issues. However, others at the meeting knew of Jean's long involvement publishing the *Guide* and of her work with Myron Avery many years ago to set the policy of not making a profit from its sale. For those who knew this history, Jean's reaction was understandable. Those attending the Maine meeting were all witness to an extremely poignant change in the management of the club, and that change overwhelmed Jean.

Up until her death on January 22, 1979, Jean Stephenson centered herself around the Appalachian Trail. Both during and beyond her long association with Myron Avery, Jean applied her knowledge, skills, and dedication to advance a project she loved. If she had her "oddities," they were the degree to which Trail work consumed her life and the insistence to avoid special recognitions for her Trail work. For nearly forty-six years, Jean was a thoroughly dedicated and competent Trail worker, because it was what she wanted to do.

Despite her avoidance of recognitions, the Potomac club officially acknowledged Jean's service by presenting her with honorary membership in 1950, and, at the April 10, 1979, council meeting, the club archives room was officially named the "Jean Stephenson Room." A simple wooden sign at the entrance to the room continues today to welcome visitors to this repository of A.T. historical documents, which includes many of Jean's Trail records, such as her numerous scrapbooks.

Following Jean's death at age 86, Ruth Blackburn was quoted in the PATC *Bulletin* of March 1979: "Without her unselfish work for the Appalachian Trail, our heritage would be poorer. Her enthusiasm inspired all who worked with her. It set a pattern for the volunteers who followed her."

The Appalachian Trail project was Jean Stephenson's life's work. She demonstrated her love for the Appalachian Trail while sitting at a typewriter, painting blazes along miles of trail, backpacking in Maine's North Woods, and organizing national conferences. She clearly enjoyed and cherished a partnership *with* Myron Avery, although she was often portrayed in this relationship as a force *behind* his success.

Nevertheless, following his death, Jean soldiered on and accomplished much in her own right, as she had for decades at his side. Her many contributions — as writer, magazine editor, Trail maintainer, event organizer, committee chairperson, advocate, and defender of the Appalachian Trail — reveal a strength of character that places her solidly within the inner circle of early Appalachian Trail leaders.

And, although she too seldom is considered among the founders of the Appalachian Trail, that honor being reserved for Benton MacKaye and Myron Avery, Jean nevertheless devoted equal skills and effort in laying the foundation of the Trail project. Jean's lifetime of work left a legacy for those men and women who continue today to preserve and enhance America's beloved Appalachian National Scenic Trail.

Ruth and Fred Blackburn in her "ATC work room" going over acquisition tract maps in the mid-Atlantic region, her starting point for seeking landowner information for both volunteer contacts and realty agents' work plans.

CHAPTER 4

RUTH BLACKBURN

1908–2004

On a rainy, overcast Sunday, November 16, 1929, Fred Blackburn took his first work trip with the two-year-old Potomac Appalachian Trail Club. Just two months short of his twenty-seventh birthday, Fred was in for an adventure. He barely knew his three companions, and he knew less about their weekend destination — a ridgetop section of the Appalachian Trail in Virginia's Blue Ridge Mountains. By many accounts, Fred was well-prepared for his current job with the Bureau of Standards at the Department of Commerce, having graduated from a prep school near Philadelphia and then Princeton University with a major in mathematics. But, he was new to the nation's capital, having moved from his family home in rural northwestern Pennsylvania just the year before, and he was definitely a newcomer to Appalachian Trail work trips.

In what was to become a life-long habit, Fred recorded the details of this weekend experience in his personal journal. The weekend began by traveling to the Blue Ridge Mountains in a Graham-Paige sedan with three other trail workers — Harold "Andy" Anderson, Charlie Thomas, and Charlie Artman. They stayed the first night in Sperryville, where the foursome attended a theater road show in a converted barn outfitted with folding chairs, a wood stove, and a simple curtain decorated with gaudy advertisements from local shop owners. As Fred recounts, "All the yokelry of the countryside and mountainside was there, having the time of its life."

The following day, they drove through the rain to Panorama, Virginia, had breakfast, and then began the challenging climb up to Mary's Rock. Apparently, the rain did not lessen Fred's introduction to trail-maintaining, for he records, "We got above the fog that hung as a low cloud over both sides of the Blue Ridge all day. There, we looked out over a sea of clouds, which presented a very novel and interesting sight." During his brief time on the ridgeline, Fred marveled at "the fluidity of the fog, and the occasional peeps we got of the landscape below" as they hiked several miles while clipping back the vegetation lining the trail's edge.

Fred's initiation to the Appalachian Trail became a fond memory, despite his recollections that the weekend adventures cost him the considerable sum of $5.50 and that, during his time in the mountains, his beloved Princeton team suffered a loss to Yale. That wet November 1929 weekend marked the beginning of Fred's long association with the Appalachian Trail project, which included decades of service to the Potomac Appalachian Trail Club and the Appalachian Trail Conference. And, in ten short months, he would marry Ruth Miller, a quiet, dark-eyed woman who would come to share his exuberance for mountain wilderness, but not then. Unlike Fred, who was quick to sign on for more work trips as well as other committee work, Ruth's interest would brew slowly over several years. Nevertheless, in time, Ruth would begin her own remarkable volunteer Trail career. The Appalachian Trail movement would capture Ruth just as sure as the view from Mary's Rock captured Fred on that rainy Sunday in 1929. And, together they would become known as the "First Couple of the Appalachian Trail."

Made chairman of Utilities & Sanitation Committee at Citizens Association Meeting and nominating committee at church. Bill got a Boy Scout uniform for $10.55. Gathering of friends at our home day after Christmas, showed slides of our trip last summer. Ruth hosts dinner party for choir.

from Fred Blackburn's diary, December 1947

THE BLACKBURN HOUSEHOLD

Ruth Elizabeth Miller was born in Reno, Nevada, in 1907. Her father was an electrical engineer who moved his family to Stockton, California, and then Portland, Oregon, where he worked for a company that was operating a trolley line. The company's promise to build them a house was slow to materialize, and the family ended up living in a tent for nearly eighteen months. The final family move was to Washington in 1913, where Ruth attended local schools and studied organ at the National Cathedral School.

Ironically, over time, Ruth's mother took a job at the Bureau of Standards, and Ruth held a six-week internship at the bureau, but there are no records that their paths ever crossed with the young mathematician, Fred Blackburn, during their time at the bureau. Rather, Fred and Ruth met through a mutual friend in the summer of 1930, and three months later — on September 6, 1930 — they were married.

Shortly after their marriage, Ruth and Fred took up residence on Conduit Road, Westgate (now Bethesda, Maryland), where they lived for ten years before moving to Allan Road. Much of what is known about everyday life in the Blackburn household is contained in Fred's journals: coal deliveries, preparations for camping trips, doctor's appointments, and weather conditions were all recorded with regularity.

The Blackburn household was quite typical of young professional families throughout the Washington area during this time period, with Fred holding a career position with the National Bureau of Standards, specializing in aeronautical instrumentation and ignition devices such as spark plugs, and Ruth serving as choir director and organist at Palisades Community Center. Later, Ruth also managed the kitchen at Westmoreland Congregational Church, and Fred served as chairman of the utilities and sanitation committee of the local citizens' association. While Fred's job required occasional trips to Detroit as a member of the Bureau of Standard's ignition research committee, and his interest in the Potomac Appalachian Trail Club took him away on weekends, Ruth chose early in their marriage to dedicate herself to community, home life, and raising their two sons, Ted and Bill.

In his daily journal, Fred describes the boys as "average in school," with Bill enjoying Boy Scouts and Ted holding down paper delivery routes in the Westmoreland Hills' neighborhood. However, as the boys grew and began joining their father on Appalachian Trail work trips and hikes, Ruth also gravitated toward outdoor activities.

Ruth's first hike on the Appalachian Trail was in Maryland, at Fred's side, and she remembered it as less than enjoyable. In a 1984 interview by the Appalachian Trail Conference's Judy Jenner, second in tenure to Jean Stephenson as *Appalachian Trailway News* editor, Ruth recalled the experience as "goshawful." The hike was held in the fall with the trail covered with leaves and very steep. Ruth could not recall the exact year. Hikers would start up and promptly slide back, until finally the hike was halted after "only a couple of miles." Ruth was not eager to repeat the experience. Although she would willingly prepare food for group work trips, Ruth's commitment to serve as church organist meant that most weekends she was not free to join Fred on hiking trips — an inconvenience that, for now, she regarded as convenient.

There's no end to the beauty of nature. No limit to its pleasure. And no better way to enjoy it than in the company of friends.

from a poster that once hung in the Blackburns' dining room.

COMING TO THE POTOMAC APPALACHIAN TRAIL CLUB

While Ruth was content to temper her involvement in Trail-related activities, Fred began to expand his involvement in the Potomac club. He was hooked, or, as he stated, "I was in my glory."

After his initiation into trail maintenance on that wet weekend in November 1929, he was sponsored into membership before year's end. Fred shared the attitude of many of the early Trail workers. The company was good, the work was no great hardship, and the exercise was beneficial. Fred was quick to lend his talent as a photographer and his skill as a handyman with tools to many club projects.

Fred became particularly active with a large, diverse group of men — from physicians to violin makers — who worked on the lean-to committee to complete a chain of three-sided shelters from Virginia to the Susquehanna River in Pennsylvania.

Through his fellow Trail workers, Fred learned of plans for the Appalachian Trail Conference's ninth general meeting to be held in August 1939 at Daicey Pond, below Katahdin in Maine. The event was to be hosted by the Potomac club, and with careful planning, Fred thought it possible to rearrange family commitments in order for Ruth and him to head to Maine for a vacation. Although Fred's Trail activities had increased steadily since becoming a member in 1929, Ruth was still contemplating membership. Quite naturally, Fred may have thought that attending the general meeting would help Ruth define her future level of involvement in the Trail community, and he wanted her experiences at Daicey Pond to have a desirable effect.

And so, Ruth and Fred approached the event as adventurers seeking to experience the Maine woods, tent camping, and new friendships. In contrast to the diligent planning that consumed Jean Stephenson for many months leading up to the meeting, Ruth was looking forward to accompanying her husband to Maine and perhaps discovering a bit more about this Trail project that had so captivated him. Jean Stephenson was working as an insider to arrange every detail from lodging to hiking, while Ruth was a casual outsider — a newcomer observing and perhaps marveling at the energy, dedication, and passion that Jean and her fellow committee members brought to every activity surrounding the meeting. They presented quite a contrast as they prepared — Ruth, relaxed and inquisitive; Jean, business-like and efficient (see page 30).

Twin Ponds Campground, then located just outside the boundary of Maine's embryonic Baxter State Park, offered a perfect setting for Fred and Ruth to be introduced to the Maine section of the Appalachian Trail and to the Trail community of passionate hikers and workers. The setting also offered a majestic view straight up Katahdin, the rugged peak that serves as the northern terminus of the Appalachian Trail. For Fred, Ruth, and their fellow campers, the view was both serene and exhilarating.

At 5,267 feet, Katahdin's summit is the destination of all northbound thru-hikers along the 2,193-mile Appalachian Trail. Thru-hikers — those who accept the challenge of completing a continuous hike of the Trail in twelve months — most often chose to travel from south to north for a variety of practical and sentimental reasons. They usually begin in early spring at the Trail's southern terminus, now on Georgia's Springer Mountain, and, for the next six months on average, they focus their daily joys and disappointments on Katahdin, a mountain whose name in the Penobscot language translates to "greatest mountain."

From the Blackburns' tent in Twin Ponds Campground, the nearby pond reflected a vision of Katahdin as real as its massive stone face and as ethereal as a thru-hiker's mixed emotions on approaching the Trail's end. Here, within the shadows of Katahdin, the Blackburns experienced the beauty of Maine and the infectiousness of the Appalachian Trail community.

We can assume that Ruth's experiences in Maine during the summer of 1939 were favorable, since the July 1940 issue of PATC's *Bulletin* announced that Ruth Blackburn had been accepted into membership. This was a major gain for the club. Further evidence of Ruth's growing interest in the outdoors is found in the October 1941 issue of the *Bulletin,* which included an article by Fred reporting on the couple's backpacking trip in the Great Smoky Mountains National Park — five days in constant rain! PATC's club records of the 1940s also reveal the Blackburns' expanding participation in club activities, with Fred serving as a member of the maps and shelters committees and Ruth joining the shelters reservation committee in 1946. However, community and family continued to be a focus of the household, as evidenced in an entry in Fred's diary in January 1947: "Ruth to choir practice; the boys to National Geographic lecture on skiing."

The Blackburn family life, for the most part, was very routine, until October 7, 1947, when Ruth was admitted to Georgetown Hospital with a fibroid tumor in her uterus. With an operation planned and Fred scheduled to provide the rare blood type Ruth needed during surgery, the seriousness of the situation was almost beyond what Fred could bear. His diary entry on October 13, following the successful removal of Ruth's tumor and appendix states, "She is still very sick from ether and in considerable distress." His devotion to Ruth is reflected in his closing comment, "I shall not say more; for — well the very thought that she might be taken away from me is enough to make every other fact or detail trivially unimportant." The next entry, dated December 5, 1947, implies a return to their usual busy, daily life. Fred happily reports, "Home from hospital October 21 — first thing was to bake some cookies for the neighborhood youngsters on Halloween." Apparently, Ruth's recovery was straining on Fred to the extent that he neglected his journal writing during the entire month of November. But, with Ruth home and her health returning, all was well once again in the Blackburn household.

May 23, 1948. Sent for a pair of hiking shoes for Ruth to L.L.Bean, mailed order Friday.

June 1-23. Intensive activity in preparation for AT conference. While I was doing this, Ruth was thinking about the food and clothing we would need....

from Fred Blackburn's diary

COMMITTING TO THE APPALACHIAN TRAIL MOVEMENT

In 1948, ATC's eleventh general meeting, the first after World War II, was held in Fontana Village, North Carolina. Fred and Ruth showed their first signs of commitment to the broader mission of the Appalachian Trail Conference at this event. At that meeting, Fred stepped up to serve in the absence of ATC's general secretary, while Ruth attended as an official PATC voting delegate. In the same year, Fred became second vice president of PATC, moving up to first vice president in 1949. Ruth continued with a somewhat more cautious increase in club activities. Fred's journal entry of January 18, 1949, hints at Ruth's growing involvement in Trail projects. Fred writes, "Ruth is down at PATC tonight helping Marion Park on something." Ruth was beginning to find her own way in the Trail community, choosing those club activities that interested her, and no longer merely tagging along with Fred.

Ruth's first leadership role in the Potomac Appalachian Trail Club began the year before as chairman of the program committee, a position she held until 1951. Likewise, Fred's involvement expanded until, in 1951, he accepted the presidency of PATC, a position he held until 1955. During Fred's presidency, Ruth began to serve on a variety of committees, most notably in 1953, when she accepted an assignment on the Myron H. Avery Memorial Fund Committee.

Avery, a charter member of PATC who served as chairman from its inception in 1927 until 1940, died suddenly on July 26, 1952, while vacationing in Nova Scotia with his son. (See page 63.) As the person most often credited with building the A.T. and providing leadership to both ATC and PATC, Avery's sudden death shocked the Trail community. Establishing a memorial fund was an appropriate way for the Potomac club to honor his legacy, and Ruth stepped up to manage the fund.

Also in the early 1950s, with Fred as president of PATC, the club took on a battle to preserve the C&O Canal as a footpath, opposing the efforts of the Bureau of Public Roads and National Park Service to convert the canal and towpath into a scenic highway. It was a long political struggle that came to a stalemate following a March 1953 public meeting.

With Fred presiding at that meeting, the assistant superintendent of the National Capital Parks unit of the National Park Service spoke enthusiastically in favor of a scenic highway rather than an over-grown, weed-infested canal, and representatives from the Audubon Society spoke of the recreational and natural values of the lands along the canal. Both Fred and Ruth recognized the need to get "boots on the ground" in order to preserve the canal and towpath as a footpath, and the boots had to have the political will to challenge the National Park Service plan. The club identified then-Associate Justice William O. Douglas of the Supreme Court, an A.T. section-hiker, as a potential advocate for their preservation position, and Fred and Ruth were actively involved in inviting Justice Douglas to hike a portion of the towpath.

As the date for the towpath hike drew near, the Blackburns brought a sense of urgency to the situation, extolling their fellow club members to assist in the logistics to provide the justice with a memorable hiking experience, and their strategy worked. Justice Douglas became a staunch advocate for preserving the towpath for recreational uses, and he willingly delivered that message to the federal agencies. Ruth recognized the value of this experience, and the "let's walk and talk" technique became one of her trademark strategies for dealing with differing views.

Comparing the various positions held by Ruth and Fred at both PATC and ATC during their most active Trail years, it becomes apparent that Fred's leadership service preceded Ruth's. However, Ruth did not work in Fred's shadow — she pursued her own interests with confidence and competency. While they would continue to work on many Trail projects together, Fred and Ruth were often regarded by fellow club members as independent teammates, supporting each other as they each pursued their own particular club interests. This unique teammate mode — together but independent — continued as Fred shifted his volunteer service to the broader Appalachian Trail Conference in 1955 by accepting a position on the board of managers. He would serve as secretary of the Conference until 1969, when Lester F. Holmes was hired as the first executive director.

Meanwhile, Ruth began to ascend the Potomac club's leadership structure. In 1959, Ruth was elected PATC's general secretary, a position she held until 1963. She was described as an "activist General Secretary" for her constant attempts to make one job do the work of two. A classic example, in which Ruth demonstrated some traits characteristic of Jean Stephenson, occurred on a hike that Ruth led for the Potomac club. After the lunchtime stop, Ruth divided the group into different sections, assigning one group the task of retracing their steps to check Trail data for inclusion in a new guidebook. Why just hike when there are Trail statistics that need to be gathered, checked, and recorded?

Although, for the most part, Fred and Ruth would continue with their separate-but-equal involvement in Appalachian Trail activities of both the Potomac club and the A.T. Conference, they participated jointly in several activities.

For example, throughout the 1950s and 1960s, both Fred and Ruth became involved in efforts to establish an organization of Pennsylvania Trail clubs. The Keystone Trails Association was born from those efforts. Fred and Ruth also worked long and hard on the construction of PATC's Anna Michener Memorial Cabin along the Pennsylvania section of the A.T. Their work from 1964 to 1966 to complete the cabin was a way to honor the close friendship that they once enjoyed with Anna. The Blackburns also continued to lead out-of-state excursions for PATC members, such as a 1965 two-week trip to Grand Teton National Park. Fred had retired in 1963 after thirty-seven years with the National Bureau of Standards, allowing him the time to organize the club trip and the opportunity to visit their son, Ted, who was then living near Jackson Hole, Wyoming.

Ruth became PATC's vice president in 1964 and then president from 1965 to 1967, a time when Fred's energies were diverted to the Appalachian Trail Conference. During her tenure as president, Ruth spearheaded PATC's efforts to establish wilderness areas in Shenandoah National Park and studied private landowner issues in the PATC regions of Virginia, Maryland, West Virginia, and Pennsylvania.

It was during those years, with Ruth serving as PATC president and Fred active as secretary of ATC, that attention was being drawn to the pressures of private landownership on the Trail's route in northern Virginia and sections of Maryland and Pennsylvania. Up until this time, much of the Appalachian Trail had been built on "gentlemen's agreements" — verbal consents for the Trail to cross private lands. Private landowners, who for decades had allowed the Trail to cross their mountain properties, were being bought out by land developers focused upon turning a profit by "taming" wilderness areas with mountaintop highways, private residences, and such business ventures as logging and mining. As developers continued to purchase mountain lands throughout northern Virginia, Maryland, and Pennsylvania, sections of the A.T. were threatened with extinction.

The Blackburns were well positioned to grasp the magnitude of development pressures on the Trail corridor, and they responded by helping to found PATC's trail-land study committee. From its inception, Ruth began to apply her signature method of "friendly persuasion" with landowners and "unflagging efforts" to preserve and protect the Trail corridor from development pressures.

Ruth's greatest service to the Appalachian Trail movement came in the years following her term as president of PATC — a period sometimes referred to as the Appalachian Trail's "government years." In the decades ahead, Ruth's service to the Appalachian Trail project would far exceed that of her husband's, and her dedication to land-ownership issues would earn her national recognition.

I hope we can move things here. Ed Garvey and I feel we have a busy future wrestling with the Trail route in northern Virginia. With the Division of Parks carrying out their program, the Trail club in the helper spot, and the National Park Service behind us, we may get a hiking trail off roads yet.

Excerpt from Ruth's letter to Richard Gibbons,
Virginia Division of Parks, February 25, 1972

Advocating for Federal Protection of the Appalachian Trail

In 1967, at Ruth's urging, PATC stood firm in an endorsement of the national trails system bill proposed under President Lyndon Johnson's administration. Ruth joined with past and present PATC presidents and ATC officers to testify before Congress in support of the bill, which would designate the completed Appalachian Trail and the to-be-completed Pacific Crest Trail as the first "national scenic trails." Their efforts were rewarded when, on October 2, 1968, President Johnson signed it into law, placing the Trail under federal protection as a unit of the national park system.

The law designated the Department of the Interior as principal administrator of the Appalachian Trail, while maintaining (in the legislative history and a later amendment) the positions of the Appalachian Trail Conference and the volunteers in its affiliated clubs in Trail management and maintenance. The law also directed the department to establish the permanent route of the Trail. According to the latter provision, the states and local governments along the Trail were given two years in which to acquire the privately owned lands along the corridor in their jurisdictions, after which time the federal government was authorized to take whatever actions were deemed necessary to complete and preserve the Trail.

Contemplating that those authorized actions included the acquisition of privately owned lands along the Trail, Ruth began to realize that her vast knowledge of land ownership surrounding the Trail in Virginia, West Virginia, Maryland, and Pennsylvania might be called upon by the park service. She was right on two counts — an aggressive land acquisition program would be needed to preserve the Trail as a continuous footpath *and* the success of such a program could be guaranteed only through acquiring a vast knowledge of who the landowners were along the Trail route.

Identifying the landowners and establishing a positive relationship with them were the first critically sensitive steps in the process of acquiring, without litigation, all the parcels needed to ensure a continuous footpath. Ruth was the right person to head this effort in the mid-Atlantic region.

By 1968, when John Oliphant assumed the presidency of PATC, Ruth was no longer burdened with the responsibilities of that position and was ready to concentrate her efforts in an area of growing personal passion — the study of landownership along the 226 miles of the Appalachian Trail that PATC maintained. With an astute understanding of the implications of the National Trails System Act, Ruth sensed the urgency for PATC to gather information on landholdings along the Trail. As she stated in her report to PATC entitled "Land Location," "When I ended my presidency in 1967, I chose A.T. land as my field of interest." Under Ruth's presidency, Oliphant had chaired PATC's land acquisition committee. Now with him installed as president, Ruth was ready to dedicate countless hours to searching courthouse records in small towns all along the Trail in Maryland, West Virginia, Virginia, and Pennsylvania.

Becoming a student of county tax maps, title searches, deeds, and other legal landowner records, Ruth was soon recognized within PATC as an expert in landownership for the A.T. from Virginia to Pennsylvania. Also stated in her "Land Location" report is a confession: "So I began what was to become a way of life. I have amassed a file drawer of notes and plats…. I have become a bore to my friends."

Ruth's passion for this work was deeply rooted in her observations of population growth and development sprawl within the region. Where landowners were once quietly content to have sections of the Trail traverse their properties with only "gentlemanly" agreements and handshakes, large tracts of mountain land were now being sold off to developers, subdivided, and then sold to individuals seeking more privacy. As these transactions increased, PATC and ATC recorded a parallel number of requests to move the Trail and to relocate shelters. In assessing this situation, Ruth identified the immediate battle to be the gathering of landownership information and not one of confronting landowners — at least not yet. The knowledge that Ruth had amassed quietly from hours spent in county courthouses quickly gained the attention of PATC, ATC, and the National Park Service. Ruth stepped with confidence into the role of Trail-lands preservationist.

During this same time period, 1967 and 1968, Fred became involved in PATC's efforts to scout and blaze an alternate route for the Appalachian Trail from Shenandoah National Park west and north to rejoin the Trail near the Susquehanna River. PATC accepted responsibility for the route south of the

Potomac River, and the Keystone Trails Association was responsible for the route north of the Potomac. The alternate route was to be blazed blue as a side-trail to the A.T. However, Fred and a small team of PATC Trail workers who set to work scouting the alternate route knew that, if private landowner issues continued to challenge the existing Appalachian Trail, their side-trail could be called into service to prevent a disruption in the Trail route.

While trail-building efforts moved forward for the blue-blazed trail, Ruth continued to "connect the dots" of privately owned parcels of land and bring urgency to their acquisition. In January 1970, Ruth published a "Report of the Trail Land Study Committee" for the years 1968 to 1969. That PATC report identified 170 owners of private land in counties throughout the four-state region of Virginia, West Virginia, Maryland, and Pennsylvania. Ruth flatly stated in the report, "First, we must know our owners." She continued her report with determination by stating, "Something good for the Appalachian Trail in northern Virginia just *must* come of this beginning."

She acknowledged that this mass of information "has come from every tax and record office in every county," and she concluded by recognizing her invaluable assistants: "Mr. Hutchinson in Loudoun County, Mr. Woods in Clarke County..." and so on until all were properly thanked. She also hinted at the enormity of the job ahead to secure the Trail route when she acknowledged that this "involves some minor political entanglement with the local jurisdictions." In the years ahead, that would prove to be a gross understatement.

While Ruth admitted that her ability to lead the Trail-preservation movement for the section of Trail from Virginia to Pennsylvania depended upon educating herself regarding landownership, she also understood that perfecting communications to landowners was just as critical. And so, she began honing her skills as a communicator. Whether engaging in face-to-face conversations with landowners, making presentations to local elected officials, or writing letters, Ruth spoke with a gentle persuasion and a strong foundation of knowledge.

Having studied the various legislative mechanisms each county and state had for accepting easements or purchasing land to secure the Trail in their jurisdictions, Ruth gained a clear understanding of what needed to be done to ensure a continuous Trail within PATC's region. Although she clearly took the lead to acquire landownership knowledge, convey information to state officials, and initiate negotiations with landowners, Ruth was also quick to acknowledge that she did not act alone. In addition to developing her skills as a communicator, Ruth's natural traits of including others and acknowledging their contributions helped to bring others to her cause. So she set about forming relationships with those living within the small communities where the Trail was being threatened and with those serving in county and state government. In addition, she carefully selected, recruited, and trained a small group of PATC members to make informal, neighborly contact with key landowners. Ruth mastered this skill of organizing support and leading team efforts. In time, she became the fulcrum between a small army of Trail supporters and county officials, state park and forest staff, and state governments.

Throughout 1970 to 1977, Ruth spent countless hours writing letters on PATC stationary and signing her letters with the title, "Assistant to the President."

Early in 1970, a continuing loss of hearing led Fred to begin withdrawing more and more from Trail activities. In contrast, Ruth's involvement was peaking. Her letter of October 25, 1973, to Charles A. McClaugherty of the Virginia Division of Parks is a classic example of the encyclopedic knowledge that she had acquired, and her chosen words show a complete absence of arrogance in the manner by which she conveys her knowledge. Ruth opened the letter with praise, "We applaud your action on Northern Virginia," and then she continued with three pages of landownership "specifics" in response to questions that were asked of her in a previous letter. She is obviously well-versed as she presents her list of eleven responses. They contain such bits of landownership information as:

"Herbert Rowe: Last year he was on an extended round-the-world trip…. Bob Cob recognized him as a former next door neighbor…ask Bob."

"Philip Dean has the land on the south side of Rt. 9…on the Loudoun Co. side."

"Louise Wilson's address I do not have. Her land I understand is incorrectly shown on the Loudoun Co. tax map…."

"Spout Run Farm is the property of James M. Folston…."

"The Game Commission…acquired land in Fauquier County as follows…."

Her stream of information becomes almost head-spinning as she closes, "PS — missed the immediate owner on #9! Daniel Burner — Appalachian Estates — Fauquier Co. 213/495 in 1961. Platted for development. 307 a. less 39 a. to the Conservation Foundation, also under Hightower. Plat enclosed."

Clockwise from top left: The Blackburns' campsite at the 1939 ATC meeting; Fred on Weverton Cliffs above the Potomac in an early, undated photograph; Ruth meeting in 1978 with federal land-acquisition officials; a 1955 photo by Ruth of Fred on a work trip; Fred and Ruth on another work trip.

Clockwise from top left: Ruth working at a desk at ATC offices; in the field; cutting the ribbon for a 1986 Trail relocation with Dave Richie, center, head of the National Park Service's A.T. Project Office, Vermont Governor Hugh Gallen, right, and Dartmouth Outing Club official David Hooke; presiding at the 1981 ATC conference in Cullowhee, N.C..

Top: Ruth and Dave Startzell, with board member Scott Johnson at right, testify before the House Appropriations subcommittee on Interior and related agencies for A.T. funding. Above, Ruth brought cakes to the ATC office and Ruth and Fred Blackburn in their garden.

Clockwise from top left: Ruth passed the chair of ATC in 1983 to Raymond F. Hunt; Hank Lautz and Charles Pugh; Fred and Ruth at a PATC party for their 50th anniversary in 1980; Charles (Chuck) Rinaldi, chief of A.T. land acquisition for the National Park Service, engages with Ruth in 1985; Ruth with NPS top acquisitions official Dick Stanton and ATC's Rima Farmer at the dedication of the Trail's bridge across the Potomac River at Harpers Ferry.

Top: The ATC board in the late 1970s, with George Zoebelein in the center at Ruth's left, past chair Stan Murray at right with envelope, Jim Botts behind him, and Ed Garvey kneeling in front of Ruth, next to Liz Levers of New York. Bottom left: Charles "Mac" Mathias, Jr., a stalwart A.T. supporter as U.S. senator from Maryland from 1969 to 1987, presented Ruth in 1979 with NPS and state commendations. Bottom right: Interior Secretary James Watt presents Ruth with the department's Conservation Service Award in 1983.

Ruth's letter not only demonstrated the vastness of her knowledge, but it was also a classic example of her graciousness. Judy Jenner, editor of ATC's *Appalachian Trailway News* from 1979 to 1999, who enjoyed a close personal friendship with Ruth, described her as compassionate, never adversarial, but able to get her point across. Those traits are evident as Ruth gently reminded McClaugherty, whom she addresses as "Chuck," that his file should already contain a letter from the Game Commission. She also was quick to admit any shortcomings on her part when she stated, "Evidently, I left out our Giles Heflin, the owner just north of Marshall."

Many officials, in addition to McClaugherty, found it difficult to keep pace with Ruth. She was truly bringing a sense of passion and urgency, not to mention knowledge, to the Trail-protection crusade. Not only was she able to master a variety of negotiating tactics, but she also developed a keen understanding of what needed to be done to gain the confidence of landowners and the respect of officials. Every step of the process, from clipping ads that appeared in local newspapers announcing land for sale to speaking before county government councils, became part of an enormous puzzle for which Ruth gained the skills needed to recognize the pieces and complete the picture.

Years later, Ruth would be recognized by Secretary of the Interior James Watt as an "authority on Trail-protection issues in northern Virginia and Maryland" and as the "single most influential volunteer in shaping the successful National Park Service Trail-protection program."

By the end of the 1980s, Ruth had dropped the use of the title, "Assistant to the President," when signing her name to official PATC correspondences. Those who received a letter from her on PATC letterhead fully knew who she was and what she represented. The recognition was well-deserved.

Dear Ruth: I have your letter of January 29 stating that I have been elected an honorary member of the Potomac Appalachian Trail Club. I consider this an honor indeed....

Benton MacKaye to Ruth Blackburn, February 3, 1968

MENDING A RIFT IN THE A.T. MOVEMENT

During the time of her transition from PATC president to chair of PATC's land-acquisition program, a correspondence began between Ruth and Benton MacKaye, originator of the Appalachian Trail concept. It was MacKaye's article, "An Appalachian Trail: A Project in Regional Planning," appearing in the *Journal of the American Institute of Architects* in October 1921, that created the seed from which the Appalachian Trail movement grew. While many within the early years of the Trail movement still viewed MacKaye as the founding father of the Trail, deeply rooted philosophical differences between Myron Avery and MacKaye on the purpose of this long trail caused MacKaye and Avery to stomp away from each other by typewriters in early 1936 and severe ties between ATC and its founder, as well as coaligned PATC.

With the stubborn, pragmatic Myron Avery serving as chairman of both PATC and ATC during the time when the federal government was supporting the development of mountaintop scenic highways that threatened to disrupt the Trail corridor, a rift developed between MacKaye and Avery. MacKaye viewed those scenic highways as incompatible with his vision for a wilderness Trail, and he staunchly opposed Avery's strategy to work with the federal government as a way of bringing additional resources to what Avery viewed as the most important and practical need — ensuring a continuous footpath as expeditiously as possible. Those fundamental differences — wilderness *versus* continuity and theory *versus* practicality — were at the heart of the rift that finally separated those two men on either side of Christmas 1935.

Following that final and fiery exchange of letters, all communications ceased between them, although, in later years, Avery allowed others in the leadership to honor MacKaye in small ways. Avery continued with all-out efforts to complete the building of the Trail, while MacKaye drifted away from the A.T. movement and into The Wilderness Society, which he and seven other A.T. pioneers in his circle had formed in 1934–35.

Ruth was positioned conveniently at PATC in the late 1960s and early 1970s to reestablish ties with MacKaye. In a letter dated January 29, 1968, Ruth informed MacKaye that he had been elected an honorary member of PATC, perhaps a first step in welcoming him back to the Appalachian Trail community. Where their first exchange of letters acknowledged Ruth as a current leader in the A.T. movement and Benton as its founding father, this relationship quickly evolved into one in which Ruth was the student and Benton the mentor. Ruth presented herself as humbled in the presence of this wise "Nestor" of the A.T. (a term first presented decades earlier by Jean Stephenson) as she sought MacKaye's advice in dealing with current Trail issues.

An example of this evolving relationship is contained in their exchange of letters in February 1968. On February 15, Ruth wrote to Benton concerning PATC's quiet efforts to push for federal legislation that would protect the Trail and give "teeth" to its land-acquisition efforts. Ruth stated, "PATC is going ahead as if nothing was brewing in Congress." She informed MacKaye of her new responsibilities as chair of "a new committee on Land Study" and her work to "first assemble names of landowners over which our section runs" — a daunting task considering that PATC was now maintaining more than 800 miles of the A.T. and its side trails.

She told MacKaye of her visits to county clerks' offices and surveying Trail land with the help of her husband, Fred. Ruth also revealed PATC's strategy to amass land-rights information quietly, not wanting to stir up any more unrest among the owners, and recognizing that "Virginians are extremely 'states rights' people and very anti-government." Although not directly seeking his advice, Ruth appeared to be reviewing this strategy with Benton, and he responded. In a letter dated February 25, 1971, Benton gave suggestions for contacting members of the Virginia legislature and offered to send a letter of support for a House bill that would protect the Trail within the state.

In addition to containing Ruth's subtle seeking of MacKaye's assistance to navigate through the politics leading up to President Johnson's signing of the National Trails System Act, their correspondence helped to reknit the A.T. movement to its founding father. While on the surface those letters appear as a straightforward exchange of information, a poignant and profound message was hidden within the words.

Signing a letter dated July 15, 1975, in a handwritten script jagged with age, MacKaye admitted to his near-blindness. Written within just five months of his death at the age of 96, MacKaye's final letter to Ruth issued a classic Yankee greeting to her and Fred and "to my other grand friends with the A.T.

fever." A relationship had been rekindled; the rift that had so long separated the A.T. movement from its founder began to close.

Those letters provide evidence that the quiet demeanor of Ruth Blackburn played a part in reuniting the Appalachian Trail project with its "Nestor," Benton MacKaye — a historic, yet quiet, event in Trail history.

Local jurisdictions and landowners are now involved and contributing their efforts toward an agreeable way for the Trail to go. With this $14.6 million appropriation for this fiscal year entirely obligated, a larger appropriation is certainly needed. We must keep up the momentum.

Statement of Ruth Blackburn to the House Appropriations subcommittee on the interior, March 6, 1979

APPALACHIAN TRAIL CONFERENCE YEARS

In 1975, Ruth was elected to the Appalachian Trail Conference's board of managers, where she was instrumental in bringing the joint influences of PATC and ATC to bear upon the federal government to provide additional funding to speed up Trail land-protection efforts.

In a 1976 letter to Commissioner Ben Bolen of the Virginia Division of Parks and others, Ruth spoke from experience when she outlined what does and does not work to improve landowner relationships. She began, "During my years as president of the [Potomac Appalachian] Club, it became clear that we did not really know who our landowners were.... We accepted the tradition that we had oral permission for the Trail. So...I began the search for owners through courthouse records. That was nine years ago." She then continued, "We now see value in overseers getting in touch with owners living on or near the land.... [This] gives the owner a sense of security." As with Charles Mc-Claugherty in 1973, Ruth found herself educating a representative of the Virginia Division of Parks, and once again she spoke with a gracious authority.

Years later, Ruth made a statement for which she was long-remembered, "I have been in Shenandoah National Park all day talking with the new park superintendent. They change so often. He is the third one I have trained." Clearly,

Ruth was willing to present her vast knowledge to state and federal officials over and over again in order to gain the desired result of Trail-corridor protection.

Although land-acquisition projects would continue to grow in complexity during her service on ATC's board of managers, Ruth's advice remained practical. When a landowner agreed to permanently locate the A.T. on his property, she urged, "Present a signed certificate, a press release to the local media, or gather family and friends for a picnic or indoor meal." Her ultimate recommendation was contained in this simple statement: "Whatever we do, let's make it mean something to the owner."

Finally, in 1978, the so-called "A.T. amendments" to the National Trails System Act authorized increased funding from $5 million to $90 million for A.T. land acquisition and *mandated* federal action to complete the acquisitions necessary to ensure a continuous trail.

The new funding came at a time when the Trail in northern Virginia from Shenandoah National Park almost to the Potomac River was under attack by private landowners. The records that Ruth accumulated from her 1970s research proved invaluable, as she spent days with federal and state officials reviewing maps and landownership records, walking sections of the Trail, identifying boundaries, and pointing out critical parcels to be acquired. Ruth became quickly recognized as the authority, with the government officials taking notes and trying to keep pace with her as she recounted the important details related to each parcel.

A resulting acquisition came early in 1980 when the 276-acre Bears Den tract in northern Virginia was purchased through the cooperative efforts of PATC, ATC, and the National Park Service. In this acquisition, as with many others, Ruth proved to be the "glue" that bound those agencies to the common goal of protecting the A.T. through a strong land-acquisition program.

The die was cast with the passage of the National Scenic Trails Act of 1968 — that like it or not the Federal Government is going to be involved in the A.T. project — and that the only hope for protecting our volunteer tradition lies in a strong, effective organization like A.T.C.... Perhaps my departure will force all of you to find a common point of agreement and a person around whom you can rally with conviction.

Charles Pugh's letter to ATC Board of Managers, September 30, 1980

NEW DIRECTIONS FOR THE APPALACHIAN TRAIL CONFERENCE

A chain of events began at a September 13, 1980, meeting of the ATC's board of managers' executive committee that disrupted leadership within the organization. For more than two weeks following this meeting, Chairman Charlie Pugh mulled over the discussions and actions of board members and struggled with a climate of "deep philosophical differences" among board members and staff. On September 30, he penned a letter notifying the Conference secretary of his resignation and alluded to business difficulties he was having with the Securities and Exchange Commission. He acknowledged the difficulty of his decision, particularly in light of the recent resignations of Vice Chairman Steve Clark and Executive Director Henry Lautz, but he implored board members to recognize "that the only hope for protecting our volunteer tradition lies in a strong, effective organization like ATC which can speak for ALL of the volunteers from Maine to Georgia." His letter contained an urgent call to "find a common point of agreement and a person around whom you can rally with conviction." That person would prove to be Ruth Blackburn.

Ruth was long recognized at PATC for her noncontroversial, inclusive style of leadership, a trait that would serve her well in the first challenging months of her chairmanship at ATC. Charlie was later to describe Ruth's ascension to chair "like pouring oil on troubled waters."

The resignations of Steve Clark and Charlie Pugh reduced the board of managers leadership to two vice chairmen, Ruth Blackburn and Jim Botts. Ruth and Jim sensed the urgency of the situation. Within four days of the date of Pugh's letter of resignation, Ruth and Jim directed their first internal correspondence to Dave Startzell and Doug Blaze. With the final words, "Good luck!" their direct 50-word memo instructed Dave and Doug to serve as acting joint directors. Ruth and Jim signed as "Co-chairmen." So, for two months following Pugh's resignation, the Conference operated under coexecutive directors Dave Startzell and Doug Blaze and cochairmen Ruth Blackburn and Jim Botts. But, if the fate of the Conference were ever in doubt, Ruth's memo of October 6 to Jim, her letter also dated October 6 to Pugh, and a joint memo from Botts and Blackburn to the board of managers, likewise dated October

6, set the pace for what Ruth expected from board and staff — a smooth, low-key transition. Collectively, those letters foretold the coming of a new era in the history of the Appalachian Trail Conference under the leadership of Ruth Blackburn, who was aptly described in the *Appalachian Trailway News'* July 2000 edition (ATC's seventy-fifth anniversary issue) as the "dynamo from Bethesda, Maryland."

Mending of the Conference's board of managers began immediately with preparations for an upcoming November board meeting. In an October 11 memo, which was signed exclusively by Ruth, she assured board members that reasonable solutions to the financial outlook were possible; that the nominating committee, under the capable direction of its chairman Chuck Sloan, would have nominations prepared to fill the board vacancies; and that the Conference's routine tasks of printing guidebooks and reviewing bylaws would continue as usual. Her closing sentences — "Our efforts must go to the future.... We will make the most of it." — hint at Ruth's natural talent for reassuring her fellow board members that the worst was past and better days were ahead.

Her earlier letter to Charlie Pugh revealed another quality — the ability to place current difficulties in a larger perspective. In this letter, she did not question or judge his decision to resign but rather showed compassion in her simple statement, "Your decision to resign must have been difficult." She also stated her intention of "going to the [board of managers] meeting with a commitment to a viable Conference which has ability to handle its own problems." She acknowledged her own transitory role in her concluding words, "Jim and I are Temporary. We can only point the way," and she invited Pugh to look to a future time when "you can once more share your talents with the A.T. community." Her well-chosen words served to calm those troubled times.

The October 6 memo also revealed what would become one of Ruth's standard modes of operating. Members were invited to arrive early for informal discussions and a hike. Her cleverly crafted invitation stated, "Let's walk and talk." The walk would be followed by another Blackburn trademark, home cooking. Informal talks, hiking, and a chili dinner were designed to ease the seriousness of the meeting's agenda. Combining food and conversation — often viewed as a female tactic — was a method that Ruth would continue to use to reassure board members and staff that together the Conference would endure those difficult times.

Ruth's series of October correspondences were meant to invite open dialogue among board members and instill confidence in their collective ability to weather the current challenges facing the Conference. And, they succeeded.

Ruth, signing as "½ Chairman," penned a separate letter on October 29 to Steve Clark welcoming his decision to return to the board of managers. After confiding, "1981 Budget has had us all on the run," she continued, "There is ample evidence that we are wide awake and ready to go." Ruth closed her letter very warmly, "I, for one, appreciate your generosity in returning to the Board. Many times you are my favorite 'devil's advocate.' We need that." In Ruth's letters, we begin to see a half-chairman with the ability to lead wholly on her own.

At the November 1980 meeting of the board of managers, Ruth accepted the chairmanship of the Appalachian Trail Conference. She brought to the position a wealth of Trail experiences, both in the field and in the meeting room — experiences that trumped her reluctance to become the first woman to assume the responsibilities of this office. As her longtime friend, *ATN* editor Judy Jenner stated, "Ruth was a reluctant chairman. She did not seek the office."

Judy further remarked, "Ruth exemplified graciousness." Jenner explained that Ruth did not alienate board members but rather invited their thoughts and participation. Ruth was noncontroversial when controversies swirled within ATC, and she exemplified a dedication to work for the good of the Conference during a difficult time in its history. Pugh remarked many years later that Ruth was the "perfect person" to succeed him. He observed, "She was noncontroversial, was respected, had a longtime involvement in the Trail project."

Coming to the position at a time when the Conference was facing significant internal challenges did not stymie Ruth's determination to tackle sensitive issues. As chairman, she began immediately by reviewing the official "Functions and Duties of Board Members," pledging to bring them up to date, and once again inviting comments from board members. Often making the seventy-five minute trip from her home to ATC headquarters in Harpers Ferry, West Virginia, three, four, and sometimes five times per week, Ruth routinely appeared at committee meetings with cookies or brownies in hand. Her offerings provided a comfortable "homespun" backdrop in which she consistently demonstrated her exceptional ability to lead ATC's board of managers. Jenner recalls that Ruth's deep-set, raccoon-like eyes were dark pools of compassion, and her smile punctuated a boundless energy. Ruth was modest, humble, and, above all, effective.

Under Ruth's chairmanship, the Conference began to regain its solid financial foundation, as evidenced in the independent audit for the years ending December 31, 1982, and 1981. Total assets increased from $470,930 to $603,234. However, the most significant gain was in the land acquisition fund, which showed an increase from just $4,839 in 1981 to $82,228 by the end of 1982. The threat of a cancellation of federal land-acquisition programs under the new Reagan administration spurred donations to ATC's newly formed land-trust program, while stronger membership drives and tighter controls by Startzell and others on internal spending accounted for the modestly improved financial posture.

"the single most influential volunteer in shaping the successful National Park Service trail protection program."

James G. Watt, Secretary of the Interior
Presentation of Conservation Service Award to Ruth Blackburn,
September 20, 1983

PROTECTING A.T. LANDS

During her three years as chairman, Ruth continued to devote time to her favorite project — protection of A.T. lands. One particular acquisition near the Trail in northern Virginia resulted in a special recognition of the Blackburns. In 1980, when PATC acquired a home with 20 acres of mountain property, planning began to create a conference and training center. With the restoration completed in 1981, a special ceremony was held to open the facility under its new name — the Blackburn A. T. Center — in honor of Fred and Ruth and their years of service to PATC and ATC. Despite such recognition, the Blackburns continued to live quietly in their two-story brick home in Bethesda.

From the outside, where more than one hundred varieties of flowers and shrubs were kept tidy but not controlled, their home reflected a simple, suburban way of life. Not so inside, particularly in the upstairs den that Fred remodeled with floor-to-ceiling shelves, work tables, and a storage closet. Everywhere were books, documents, maps, mementos, an old typewriter, and telephone. The activities that occurred in this room went well beyond traditional suburban living. Here, Fred had created an efficient working space and dubbed it Ruth's A.T. office (see page 72). The Blackburn den was not a place for sipping coffee and discussing classical literature. Rather, the room was a reflection of Ruth, who she was and what was important to her. It was a place for research, examination, and reflection of all things Trail-related. Those privileged to enter this space immediately sensed a quiet pride from the woman who knew its entire contents. And, they were similarly struck by the depth of her commitment to the A.T. project.

Beginning in 1981, assisted by board, staff, volunteers, and representatives from a legion of partners, Ruth spearheaded the project to create an ATC land trust. Following months of planning and countless letters, on July 22-23, 1982, an A.T. Land Trust Workshop welcomed twenty-two agencies to the Pocono Environmental Education Center at Dingmans Ferry, Pennsylvania. The workshop was designed to spearhead serious discussions about the feasibility of the Appalachian Trail Conference establishing a land trust specifically to protect and provide for the future of America's long trail. Prior to the workshop, a February 1982 memo by Dave Richie, manager of the Park Service's Appalachian Trail Project Office, confessed that, "Ruth Blackburn is wrestling mentally with the issues involved with setting up an ATC land trust."

However, just two months after the workshop, Ruth sent out a series of letters inviting a select number of people to serve on a newly formed A.T. land trust committee. All reluctance was gone, and Ruth was comfortable with her decision to proceed. Here was evidence of a Conference removed from crisis, able to tackle new projects, and capably led by its first woman chair.

In addition to establishing that committee, several special projects occupied Ruth's time and talents during her tenure as chair of ATC. One of those projects was serving as chair and secretary of the Maryland A.T. Committee, an informal group of key partners. To strengthen ATC's internal structure, Ruth focused her efforts and the efforts of staff and board on creating a personnel policy manual. And, to secure the Conference's future, she supported efforts to expand ATC's marketing strategies.

Most notably, Ruth was a politically active spokesperson for the Appalachian Trail. When President Ronald Reagan and his administration imposed a moratorium on all federal land-acquisition funds in 1981 and 1982, in effect hobbling ATC's acquisition efforts and provoking the formation of its land-trust program, Ruth was ready to speak up and speak out. With a reassuring voice, she testified before congressional committees in an effort to reverse Reagan's actions. From many years of studying landownership along the A.T. and tireless efforts to urge acquisition of key parcels to protect the A.T. corridor, Ruth was well-qualified to speak about the importance of federal appropriations to continue land-acquisition projects.

In addition to demonstrating her own knowledge and experience in the area of landowner negotiations, Ruth was able to raise the National Park Service's level of confidence in ATC's ability to manage the Trail. Here, she was a well-respected spokesperson for the Conference's vast, well-organized, and growing volunteer network of maintaining clubs. From this confidence sprang the 1984 signing of a new A.T. cooperative management agreement, which delegated management and maintenance of lands acquired by the National Park Service for the Trail securely in the hands of ATC and its team of volunteer-driven maintaining clubs.

In gaining the respect of the National Park Service and other federal agencies for her work, Ruth was able to impart this respect to ATC and the Trail. This respect became her greatest legacy.

---

*I just have a few postmortem comments about this weekend meeting....
This is the first meeting that I have ever attended in over seven years of going
to these meetings in which I felt that the group acted like a board entrusted to
manage an organization.... This is a watershed development. It ensures the
ATC can control its own destiny and indeed, even has a destiny...made possible
by the degree of respect and trust which has been built up rapidly through your
administration as executive director and Ruth's leadership as chairman.*

**Corresponding Secretary Charles Sloan to
Executive Director Laurence Van Meter, April 19, 1982**

NATIONAL SERVICE AWARD

Following her three years of service as chair of ATC, Ruth continued to serve as a chair emeritus. Her general involvement in the A.T. community consisted of serving on board committees, overseeing the Bears Den Hostel, and meeting with federal agency representatives on land-acquisition projects.

A high-water mark in Ruth's service to the A.T. community occurred on September 20, 1983, when the Department of the Interior recognized her with a Conservation Service Award, the department's highest civilian honor. As described in the National Park Service's November 1983 *Courier*, "The crowd was standing-room only, the auditorium awash with waves of appreciative applause," as Ruth shared the limelight with four Distinguished Service Award recipients and twenty-one Valor Award recipients. Interior Secretary James G. Watt presented the awards.

The citation presented to Ruth begins, "In recognition of her outstanding contribution in the protection and management of the Appalachian National Scenic Trail," and continues, "The respect that Ms. Blackburn commands throughout the Appalachian Trail community has been a principal source of confidence in the leadership of the Appalachian Trail Conference, which recently culminated in the decision of the National Park Service to entrust the Conference with management responsibility for lands it has acquired for the Appalachian Trail."

Ironically, Interior Secretary James Watts was known as a long-standing opponent of federal land-acquisition programs, yet perhaps unintentionally he "inspired" much of the growth in ATC's lands fund and other programs.

This honor was followed by the signing of that A.T. delegation agreement on January 26, 1984. All the responsibilities for those Trail lands that a federal park staff would traditionally have, except law enforcement and certain compliance with other federal laws, were transferred to ATC under an agreement that has been renewed continuously since its original signing. Thus began an enhanced partnership between the federal government and the volunteer-based, nonprofit Appalachian Trail Conference — known since 2005 as the Appalachian Trail Conservancy.

Signed by ATC Chair Raymond F. Hunt and National Park Service Director Russell E. Dickenson, this agreement upheld the spirit of the amended National Trails System Act. It also reaffirmed the federal government's confidence in ATC's ability to manage the Trail and its protected lands in the public interest and to the same level as a national-park staff. Many would maintain that the "seed" from which that confidence grew originated with Ruth's quiet courthouse visits and rested firmly upon the leadership she so aptly demonstrated.

In the late 1980s, Fred's health began to deteriorate as he struggled with dementia. Following his death in 1990, Ruth continued alone with her Trail activities. In May 1994, she received another national recognition when the third national conference on national scenic and national historic trails nominated her to the honor roll of people essential to the creation of the national trails system. That would become a final salute to this remarkable woman.

In the fall of 1995, while walking on Washington's Capital Crescent Trail, Ruth was struck by a bicyclist and suffered a broken hip. While not life-threatening, the injury aggravated her own growing loss of memory. In the spring of 1996, her son, Bill, insisted that she relocate to his home in Prescott, Arizona. From afar, Ruth remained interested in ATC's projects and connected to the many friends she had made within the Trail community. When on January 3, 2004, Ruth Elizabeth Blackburn died at the age of ninety-six, her remarkable years of service to the Appalachian Trail came to a close.

Ruth's involvement in the Appalachian Trail project mirrored the changing role of women in the last century. She was first a housewife and mother, who supported her husband's early interest in the activities of the local Potomac Appalachian Trail Club. When their children were well along in school, Ruth increased her participation in Trail activities. Ruth and Fred shared many happy experiences hiking, maintaining the A.T., remodeling shelters, helping to form other Trail clubs, and traveling.

Within this loving relationship, Ruth came into her own — gaining knowledge of Trail issues, honing decision-making skills, and assuming more and more leadership roles within the Potomac club and the Conservancy.

And, beyond this loving relationship, she went on to surpass Fred's contributions to the A.T. project. She became active in national issues affecting the Appalachian Trail, not hesitating to become an official spokesperson for the Appalachian Trail Conference and defender of the Trail.

Ruth is perhaps best remembered for bringing a national credibility to the Appalachian Trail Conference. Her leadership provided a strong pivotal point upon which the Conservancy was able to redirect its staff, board, member clubs, and volunteers to serve a core mission to preserve, protect, and maintain the Appalachian Trail.

Ruth earned the acclaim of all those within the A.T. movement as being a leader capable of engaging in what Benton MacKaye labeled the "magnificent fight" — and she did it magnificently.

Hikers relax in perhaps the 1940s at an Appalachian Trail shelter in northern Virginia, the section where Ruth Blackburn first focused her land-protection efforts.

Challenges to the footpath...appear at times overwhelming and require end-less meetings, feasibility studies, forest plans, all for a group of volunteers who enthusiastically cut weeds, paint blazes, and build shelters.

from Chair's Message, *Appalachian Trailway News,*
September/October 1994

CHAPTER 5

MARGARET DRUMMOND

1922–2015

Margaret Drummond had a way of straddling a log, pulling firmly on a debarking tool to strip its bark, and then tossing her head back to show the most pleasant smile. Those motions would be performed over and over, as she concentrated on preparing the log for placement in the rising wall of an Appalachian Trail shelter.

As a participant in a Georgia Appalachian Trail Club (GATC) work party, Margaret had shouldered her tools up the mountain earlier in the day, helped with the selection of just the right trees to fell for the day's construction project, and worked throughout the morning debarking a sizable stack of logs. She most likely looked forward to joining her fellow workers for a lunch that offered a spectacular view from one of Georgia's mountaintops. To Margaret Drummond, this was a perfect day spent in a perfect way.

Margaret Drummond, left, during a break at the 1986 club presidents' meeting. Dave Startzell is at right, holding the umbrella.

Margaret's dedication to Trail maintenance, to inviting others to join in work trips, and to organizing workshops aimed at improving Trail-maintaining skills was soon recognized throughout the A.T. community. In time, she was welcomed into governance positions in the Georgia Appalachian Trail Club and the Appalachian Trail Conference, where she earned accolades for being forthright, visionary, analytical, and inclusionary. And, in time, her Trail work became a life's work that spanned more than forty years.

Margaret Drummond has built a reputation based on sound knowledge and hard work.

Friendships of the Trail, History of the Georgia
Appalachian Trail Club, 1981-1990

ATLANTA IS MY HOME

Margaret Drummond described herself in an interview as being "accidentally" born in Tulsa, Oklahoma. The date was December 4, 1922. She lightheartedly explained that, although she lived almost all of her life in Atlanta, Georgia, and therefore considered herself an "Atlantan," she was not native-born. At the time of her birth, Margaret's family had relocated to Tulsa, where her father found employment to support a growing family. So it happened, according to Margaret, much by accident that she was born far from the city that she always called home, Atlanta.

Oklahoma in the 1920s did not offer young Margaret many memorable outdoor experiences beyond an occasional family picnic. In fact, her earliest recollections of family life in Oklahoma were tinged with the alienation her parents experienced as third-generation Atlanta natives transplanted to a land of sod houses and sodbusters. Gone were Atlanta's gracious homes and tree-lined streets, replaced by the farmer's plow and miles of flatland. However, by the time Margaret reached school age, the family had returned happily to Atlanta.

Margaret settled right in, graduating from Girls High, receiving a bachelor's degree in biochemistry from Agnes Scott College in Decatur, Georgia, and a master's degree, also in biochemistry, from Emory University. She then faced a crossroads in her education. Although she was interested in continuing her studies at Emory, at the time the university did not offer a doctoral program in microbiology. Consequently, Margaret interrupted her studies and accepted a position in the Tuberculosis Research Laboratory, first with the Centers for Disease Control in Atlanta and later with the Veterans Administration, also in Atlanta.

When the research laboratory relocated to Washington, Margaret was offered a position working under a prominent tuberculosis expert in Chapel Hill, North Carolina. Accepting this position meant leaving Atlanta, but a move to Chapel Hill held the promise of entering a doctoral program in microbiology at the University of North Carolina. Margaret chose to relocate to Chapel Hill. However, after just one year, Margaret's research work and studies were interrupted by family problems that necessitated her return to Atlanta. Fortunately, during her short absence from Atlanta, Emory instituted a doctoral program in microbiology, and Margaret quickly enrolled. She now enjoyed her chosen course of study and her chosen hometown.

This time, her return to Atlanta was permanent. Margaret's work at Emory's School of Medicine would span thirty years, first as a doctoral student and then as a professor and researcher. However "accidental" she may claim her birth to have been in Tulsa, her residency in Atlanta was both deliberate and desirable.

Academic life at Emory suited Margaret well, and she dedicated much of her time to teaching, lecturing, and writing. When Margaret was in her mid-thirties, a close friend, Mary Louise Wilcox, moved from Atlanta to Denver. Over a series of summers in the 1950s, Mary Louise invited Margaret to step outside her academic world of classrooms and laboratories and come to Colorado. Margaret accepted, and together they enjoyed canoeing, rafting, and camping trips throughout the West. Margaret's appreciation of the natural world peaked during a canoe trip through Minnesota's Boundary Waters, after which she went on to canoe several rivers in Colorado and Georgia.

Earlier, about the time that Margaret became well-established as associate professor of microbiology at Emory, another friend, Lee Perry, extended an invitation to join him for a hike on the Appalachian Trail. With this invitation, a whole new world of the outdoors opened for Margaret.

It looks like the best thing we can do is to go ahead and secure members and hold a meeting at some early date and complete the organization. I suggest that for the present that we select only those persons who have shown enough interest to indicate they are really going to do some hiking. We want as little dead wood as possible in the organization.

Eddie Stone letter to Charlie Elliot, October 15, 1930

DISINTERESTED HIKER TO ACCOMPLISHED HIKE LEADER

Margaret's first experience with the GATC did not leave a favorable impression on her. She recalls being in her late twenties, when she decided to attend an outing during which it rained all weekend and "there was mud in the spaghetti." Looking back, she attributed some of her unpleasant reaction to being city-reared and a real novice hiker. And so, several years passed before she was inclined to repeat the experience.

When another friend and long-time GATC member, Pat Bell, convinced Margaret to go on a club hike one more time, the experience was more positive. Margaret finally joined the club in 1961. She soon discovered that her university experiences had prepared her to contribute to the committee work of the club, and likewise her love of canoeing adventures morphed into a love for Trail work. The Georgia club, needing both committee workers and Trail maintainers, enthusiastically welcomed her.

Margaret soon became active in a variety of club activities, spurred by her realization that the planning that took place during Trail committee meetings was much more exciting than the usual dry agendas of the university. She was also captivated by the strong bonds that developed among Trail workers who painted blazes, cleared blow-downs, and built new trails. Referred to in the Georgia club as "Friendships of the Trail," such relationships began to form an important part of Margaret's social life outside the university.

Margaret joined the GATC in 1961, but it was not until November 1966 that she led a club activity. The club's annual fall trip to the Dillard Farm was scheduled for November 4-5, and, as leader, Margaret was most likely schooled by some of the long-standing members of the club as to the many traditions that should be followed during the weekend visit to the farm.

Those traditions, going back as far as 1933, included a truck ride to near the top of Rabun Bald, where, each year, Mrs. Dillard welcomed the group to one of the biggest dinners ever set before them. The meal often exceeded an astonishing nine courses, finished off with pitchers of homemade cider. Mrs. Dillard, who was known for her storytelling of the early history of Dillard House and the early inhabitants of the Georgia mountains, also provided the entertainment. As with many A.T. maintaining clubs, the GATC held fast to such traditions, and Margaret's willingness to lead the annual trip to Dillard House indicated that she, too, placed a value on club traditions.

Twenty-two fellow hikers joined Margaret for the 1966 trip, which included moonlight hikes and plenty of time for socializing. As leader, Margaret assumed responsibilities for arranging transportation, food, accommodations, and activities — all the while enjoying a mountain retreat that differed greatly from her daily university life. We can assume that the weekend held its challenges, but, for Margaret, it was most likely a refreshing change from the class-room and lecture-hall environments.

Nineteen-sixty-six was also a time for club membership to face some serious threats to the A.T. in Georgia. For the past five years, the ATC and the Georgia club anguished over the federal government's slow but sure progress toward extending the Blue Ridge Parkway through Georgia, a project that was expected to cause a relocation of most of the Appalachian Trail off the ridgeline. Now, attention shifted to a related threat within the Smoky Mountains National Park. At a GATC-sponsored multiclub meet, which traditionally brought together the southern A. T. maintaining clubs to discuss common interests and issues, it was decided to hold a protest hike against the transmountain highway and in favor of the incorporation of the national park into the protected wilderness system. And so, the Georgia club joined with the Smoky Mountain Hiking Club and Carolina Mountain Club to plan the "Save-Our-Smokies Wilderness Hike" in October 1966.

The event drew an astounding five hundred and seventy-six registrants, with two hundred and thirty-four hikers completing the seventeen-mile protest hike. A conflict with another scheduled hike limited participation by members of the Georgia club to just eighteen. Although club records do not identify those eighteen hikers, and therefore we do not know if Margaret was among the protestors, their experiences supporting neighboring A.T. clubs to oppose this mountaintop highway would prove valuable to the Georgia club in future years.

Margaret did not lead a club activity again until March 1968, when she led a two-day hike from Cooper Gap to Woody Gap attended by twenty-three members. In the same year, the club drew upon Margaret's academic skills by electing her editor of the club's newsletter, *The Georgia Mountaineer*. At that time, the editor held a voting position on the board of directors. However, new leadership within the club would soon eliminate Margaret's ability as editor to vote on issues brought before the board and challenge many of the founding principles and traditions of the club.

Assuming for the moment that the decision will be made NOT to extend the Parkway into Georgia, who will decide the location of the Georgia Trail?... I would like to request of you that the Clubs be permitted a voice in that decision.

Margaret Drummond letter to David Richie, May 1, 1977

FEDERAL GOVERNMENT ISSUES PERSIST

Also in 1968, two actions by the federal government greatly affected the future status of the Appalachian Trail — one of long-term benefits, the other to become a persistent threat. On October 2, 1968, President Lyndon Johnson signed the National Trails System Act. The act designated the Appalachian Trail and the to-be-finished Pacific Crest Trail as the first components of a national system of recreational and scenic trails. As a result of that legislation, the Appalachian Trail was renamed — for official documents — the Appalachian National Scenic Trail and its management fell under the Department of the Interior (in official cooperation with the Department of Agriculture), which assigned it to the National Park Service. In time, the Appalachian Trail came to be considered an official "unit" of the national park system.

The Georgia club, along with other maintaining clubs, welcomed federal protection of the Trail with some reservations. Volunteer Trail maintainers from Maine to Georgia, who were for the most part an independent lot, began to question, Would federal protection of the Trail come at the cost of government interference with the way volunteers had been maintaining the Trail for years? Stanley Murray, then chair of ATC, wrote reassuringly in response to the passing of this act, "We expect that most of the present arrangements for maintenance of the Trail by clubs and private individuals will be continued." Such statements offered a level of reassurance but little guarantee that tensions would not develop between veteran volunteer Trail maintainers and national park staff.

Then, on October 9, 1968, the Blue Ridge Extension Parkway bill was finally passed, giving life to a long-threatened project to extend the Blue Ridge Parkway south into Georgia. Passage of the bill created a flurry of activity within the Georgia club. While work to identify and blaze an alternate route had been rather slow and cautious, trail crews within the GATC quickly mobilized into action with the passing of this bill. Flagging of a reroute now became of paramount importance in order to avoid a disruption of the Trail.

Unforeseen at the time, the parkway bill would continue to haunt the Georgia club and ATC well into the 1990s. As late as August 1993, David Sherman of the USDA Forest Service inquired of the National Park Service whether the parkway project still lingered on the federal government's authorization list. While the response was, "Yes, legally, the parkway could be extended," Dave admitted that, practically, the public climate would not allow it. However, at the time of the passing of the 1968 bill, the threat that many miles of the A.T. in Georgia would soon be displaced seemed real and eminent. Consequently, the Georgia club prepared to respond with a sense of urgency, understandably not knowing that the parkway-extension issue would smolder for years.

GATC records note the irony of President Johnson's signing the National Trails System Act in the same year that Congress passed a bill jeopardizing the Georgia section of this newly christened Appalachian National Scenic Trail. According to an article in the November 2005 issue of *The Georgia Mountaineer,* "Spotlight on Margaret Drummond," by Shelley Rose, Margaret described the 1968 events as "an exciting time with all this happening. We couldn't just lop weeds; we needed to do everything." Her words contain a sense of urgency directed toward the Trail's maintaining clubs and their volunteer workers that trail work may be held to different standards and subjected to new regulations under Johnson's act. Margaret was quick to grasp the possible ramification of this federal legislation, and she was cautiously energized by what lay ahead for the GATC.

As 1968 drew to a close, the entire GATC leadership became engaged in the parkway extension issue, dedicating many hours preparing for a possible relocation of the Georgia section of the A.T. At the same time, and in response to the passing of the National Trails System Act, Margaret began to seriously consider the effect this legislation might have on the maintaining clubs and volunteer maintainers. Perhaps she possessed an uneasy foreboding that, without introducing a level of professionalism into the way volunteers performed Trail maintenance, the federal government would take over these responsibilities and the role of the maintaining clubs would be seriously diminished. To avert such a threat to the role of volunteers, Margaret's commitment to Trail maintenance and to the training of Trail maintainers increased.

As Margaret's level of involvement in the Georgia club increased in the coming years, she would find herself in a position to secure both the role of volunteer maintainers and the original route of the A.T. through Georgia. And, in retrospect, it can be said that in these two areas — professionalizing the maintenance performed by volunteers and bringing to a conclusion the many years of uncertainty surrounding the official route of the Trail through Georgia — Margaret would leave her greatest marks in A.T. history.

Club activities in 1969 were largely focused on responding to the events of 1968. The first challenge was determining the club's response to the federal government threat to extend the Blue Ridge Parkway through Georgia. As editor, Margaret featured an article by outgoing GATC President Ed Seiferle in the December 1968 bulletin on what he dubbed the club's "Big Trail Relocation Project." The challenge, he explained, was more than deciding upon a reroute of the Trail in Georgia. In fact, the National Trails System Act required that the exact route of the Trail and the associated rights-of-way be selected, described, and recorded in the *Federal Register* — a task that was seriously complicated by the parkway bill. Should the club declare the Trail's present route as the official route, thereby ignoring the parkway threat? Or face the uncertainties of perhaps as many as 50 miles of the 76 miles of present A.T. in Georgia being displaced by a parkway extension and actively seek a preferred alternative route?

The club's choice became clear on a cold, foggy, rainy January weekend, when twenty-six club members and guests joined a team from the Forest Service to place thirty-five panels marked with white X's along a newly proposed reroute of the Trail. The project concluded in late January with aerial photography of the proposed reroute cleverly guided by the bright white X's. Both the Georgia club's bulletin and the ATC newsletter acclaimed the success of the project, noting that, despite cold, rain, and fog, the GATC membership responded with a huge amount of team spirit. An alternative route was marked, photographed, and mapped; the Forest Service agreed to construct the rerouted Trail; and the long wait for a parkway extension began.

The second issue facing the Georgia club in 1969 centered on the 1968 signing of the National Trails System Act, which mandated the formation of a new advisory council. By late spring 1969, the secretary of the interior completed appointments to this council, which to the satisfaction of GATC members included sound Georgia representation. Club member Henry Morris, who was also serving on the ATC board of managers, accepted a position on the new council, as did Georgia State Park's Robin Jackson.

By 1969, Margaret appeared sufficiently comfortable in her role as newsletter editor to make some cosmetic changes to *The Georgia Mountaineer* and the way it was produced. Beginning with the July issue, Margaret instituted new printing and reproduction processes that provided a more readable and presentable appearance of the newsletter at a reduced cost. In addition to using an off-set printing process, *The Georgia Mountaineer* would now be printed in green ink — radical changes for a hiking club!

We in GATC are fortunate and proud to call Margaret one of our own.

Shelley Rose in *The Georgia Mountaineer,* November 2005

FINDING A HOME WITHIN THE GATC

While Margaret's cosmetic changes to *The Georgia Mountaineer* were made with confidence and met with over-all success, the same cannot be said for several changes within the GATC being made under club president Jim Cooger. In fact, many founding principles of the club appeared to be under siege in

1969. Soon after taking office, Cooger succeeded in effecting a change in the official purpose of the club. Primarily founded to bring together people who shared a common interest in hiking and in building and maintaining trails for hiking, specifically the Appalachian Trail, Cooger urged for a broader mission: to educate the public on ecological and environmental conservation of Georgia's natural areas. To do so, he supported participation in GATC activities by the general public.

Early in his presidency, new bylaws were also adopted that expanded the categories of membership to five, with two categories of membership consisting of persons who would make financial contributions to the club in amounts fixed by the board. This change reflected Cooger's interest in reaching beyond the current membership to seek additional funds to support his broader mission. Oddly, the new bylaws also eliminated the newsletter editor from the board of directors. Margaret now found herself removed from club governance.

Club records are silent regarding any reaction from Margaret, as she was stripped of her voting position on the board, but the records are quite clear in reporting the opposition many club members expressed for the direction Cooger was leading the GATC. Slowly, club leadership began to unravel, as many longtime members viewed Cooger's actions as counter to the club's traditional emphases on friendships, hiking, and stewardship of the Appalachian Trail.

On October 4, 1969, Margaret was involved in her own club fray. Apparently, she had volunteered to lead a hike that the GATC board of directors advertised to the general public. Planned as a way to publicize the club and increase its membership — priorities under Coogler's leadership — the event succeeded in attracting more than fifty guest hikers. But, when only a small handful of seasoned club hikers showed up to assist Margaret, the logistics of transporting the guest-hikers to the Trail and shepherding them the full distance of the hike became very problematic. Determined to call attention to the difficulties she faced, Margaret boldly used the club bulletin to express her displeasure, and she did not hold back. In the October issue of *The Georgia Mountaineer*, she explained that the board of directors, in an effort to increase membership, had decided to publicize this one club event to the public on an experimental basis. Unfortunately for Margaret, the expectation that club members would show up to assist with the hike proved to be naïve and wrong. To admonish her fellow club members, Margaret featured a photograph of the group in the newsletter along with the caption, "Where are the GATC members?"

She further painted a clear picture of disorganization by suggesting that the fifty guest hikers appeared *blue*, because they were longing for the assistance of club members with the car shuttle and with keeping the crowd from straggling on the Trail. In her article, Margaret then proposed that the guest hikers turned *white*, as they paled before an array of 23-odd cars with disoriented drivers transporting the crowd to the start of the hike. She grudgingly labeled herself a "harried hike leader," but her deepest regret was the public's perception of the club as having a lack of organization and efficiency.

Although Margaret handled her responsibilities as hike leader exceptionally well, she made her point that chaos results and the club's image suffers when a hike leader does not have the support of fellow club members. On the surface, Margaret's challenge in handling this large group of guest hikers was due to the absence of support from fellow club members. But, a deeper cause was soon identified, as many club members turned their scrutiny toward a club president bent on opening the club and its events to a general public that may be ill-prepared to participate. By recounting her "harried hike leader" experience in the club newsletter, Margaret most likely lent support to those club members who preferred the small, friendly club atmosphere over Coogler's open invitations to the general public. Absent in his efforts to grow the club through increased publicity was the forethought of how club volunteers such as Margaret would deal with large groups of guest hikers.

When Cooger continued to open club events to the general public, to place an emphasis on fund-raising, and to divert the club away from its core mission to maintain the Georgia section of the Appalachian Trail and toward broader environmental issues, a representative group of club members prepared to voice opposition to the board of directors. By the November 4th board meeting — just one month since Margaret's over-taxing experience — that group called for a reversal of these trends and a return to the traditional hiking fellowship that the membership had long enjoyed. In their presentation to the board, the group demanded curtailing the widespread, public recruiting of new members and returning the club's primary focuses back to maintaining the Appalachian Trail and supporting ATC and its programs. The bulletin editor also was to be restored to a voting position on the board.

By year's end, the board reversed many of Coogler's initiatives and appointed a special committee to solicit opinions from all club members and then make recommendations to the board. Within a few short months, the board conceded to all the committee's demands. The result was a redirecting of the GATC back to its founding principles. Soon, the general membership was again enjoying a spirited friendship and a strong commitment to the Appalachian Trail.

At year's end, Margaret was elected club historian, regaining a solid voting position on the board that she would hold through 1971. Nevertheless, Margaret would long remember her "harried hike leader" experience and use the lessons learned to guide her as she moved through the ranks of the Georgia club and then the ATC. Many of her longtime Trail friends recalled that Margaret would often sit at the front of the bus on club-sponsored excursions, just so she could welcome newcomers as they climbed on board. She was always welcoming to guest hikers, and she prepared herself to respond to their possible unpreparedness. In doing so, Margaret welcomed newcomers while also holding fast to the intimate friendships enjoyed among longtime club members. Projecting a friendly confidence to all guest hikers would become her tool for recruiting new members who shared the GATC's love for the outdoors, the environment, and most notably the Appalachian Trail.

As 1969 came to a close, club leadership was once again in sync with its membership, and Margaret was finding a home within the Georgia hiking community. In addition to enjoying a secure position on the Georgia club's board of directors by serving as club historian, she continued to regularly lead club hikes and multiday trips. She also was prepared to become involved in the larger Appalachian Trail project, as evidenced by her accepting an appointment in early 1970 as editor of ATC's guidebook to the Smokies, Nantahalas, and Georgia.

In October 1970, Margaret again attracted a crowd for a club hike, but this time a more balanced group of 31 guests and 21 fellow members joined her for a hike from Blue Ridge Gap down Hightower Creek. A 1971 excursion on Sarah's Creek and a 1972 weekend canoe trip on the Chattahoochee River canoe trip gave Margaret the opportunity to share her interest in canoeing with fellow club members. With each successful experience, Margaret became more recognized for her outdoor leadership skills, and this well-earned reputation within the Georgia club fostered Margaret's desire to expand her experiences within and beyond the Georgia club.

In 1971, the official route of the Appalachian Trail finally was published in the *Federal Register,* as mandated by the National Trails System Act. Since the official route now included the reroute of the Trail in Georgia, Margaret, as editor, presented the reroute alignment as the official route in the ATC guidebook. Although this gave the appearance that the route was finally and officially settled, in reality, ambiguity would continue to haunt the Georgia club for more than a decade.

From 1972 to 1974, Margaret served as a director-at-large on the GATC's board of directors, leading club hikes each year. After leaving the board and reducing her club activities in 1975, her involvement in the club rebounded in 1976 as she accepted the demanding position of trail supervisor. This assignment saddled her with many responsibilities: organizing work trips, training new and seasoned trail maintainers, and filing reports on trail conditions. Much of this work centered on the Georgia section of the Appalachian Trail, but it also included many other trails throughout the state that the GATC maintained. Margaret flourished in this role, with many of the club records reflecting her increased commitment to and sheer enjoyment of trail maintenance. In addition to coordinating and recording the club's trail-maintenance activities, Margaret led trail-maintenance work days in March with 52 participants and in July with 13.

Then, in 1977, having become a well-seasoned hike leader and Trail maintainer, as well as an accomplished committee member, Margaret was elected president of the GATC. As only the second woman to step into the role of president, Margaret came to this leadership position with an understanding of the value members placed on club traditions and comradery. She shared the club's core mission to maintain, protect, and promote the Appalachian Trail. And, most importantly, she was able to accept the presidency confident that her work on the Trail and in committees had earned her the respect and friendship of club members, both men and women.

As she stepped into the role of GATC's president, Margaret was able to capitalize on several personal traits often regarded as feminine, such as promoting inclusion, partnerships, and consensus. As we shall see, those qualities became Margaret's strengths as she expertly led the GATC, and eventually the ATC, through the intricacies of strengthening a three-party cooperative-management system to support the Trail.

Since joining the GATC in 1961, Margaret had led hikes and work trips — some successfully and some with long-remembered challenges. She had served on committees and under several club presidents — some highly popular and some less so. And, above all, she was ready to become more engaged. So, in 1977, Margaret understandably began referring to the Georgia club as "my club," emphasizing her sense of belonging to the club rather than ownership of the club. Margaret had become one with its mission, work, and membership. The GATC was "her club."

Margaret cemented the relationship between the Club, the Conference and the Forest Service. This was a turning point for the GATC.

Rosalind Van Landingham in *The Georgia Mountaineer*,
November 2005

AT THE HELM OF THE GATC

As president of the GATC, Margaret quickly began to steer the club's top priorities toward maintenance and preservation of the Appalachian Trail. She supported the preservation of wilderness and conservation of natural resources, but she would actively engage the club in those issues only to the extent that the disregard of these issues posed threats to Georgia's hiking trails, particularly the Appalachian Trail.

Such was the case when, during her first year as president, Margaret tackled the persistent issue that had direct consequences for the preservation of Georgia's wilderness — the extension of the Blue Ridge Parkway into Georgia. She attempted, with little results, to bring attention to this nagging issue by writing to Dave Richie, manager of the National Park Services' A.T. Project Office, requesting information on who would make the decision as to whether this project would go forward or be officially abandoned. She received advice that either the Georgia club or ATC should send an official letter to the Department of the Interior requesting the reinstatement of the original white-blazed Trail as the official route. She also learned that a Georgia law authorizing the extension of the parkway through the state stood in the way of reinstating the original route and would have to be rescinded. Her efforts were shedding light on the complexities of the parkway issue and making it apparent that any request by the Georgia club or ATC could, at best, ever so slowly move the federal government to take action.

Nineteen-seventy-seven was also a year for club ceremonies. In April, Margaret joined with four pioneer members of the GATC to unveil a new historical marker in Amicalola Falls State Park at the beginning of the approach trail to the southern terminus of the Appalachian Trail. Another ceremony occurred in November to commemorate the long-awaited completion of the Toccoa River Bridge. President Margaret Drummond and Forest Service Supervisor Pat Thomas officially cut the ribbon on November 5 (see page 131). This event marked the completion of the Loop Trail, which was primarily comprised of the old white-blazed A.T. and its proposed reroute. It also marked a partnership between the Georgia club and the Forest Service that was nurtured by a longtime friendship between Margaret and Pat Thomas.

As president of the GATC, Margaret made a concerted effort to promote activities that strengthened the club's ties to ATC. For example, she invited members of the Conference's board of managers to speak at GATC meetings and encouraged her fellow members to participate in various activities of the Conference. Perhaps sensing the importance of the evolving partnership among the ATC, federal agencies, and the maintaining clubs, Margaret set about nurturing the relationship between her club and the ATC.

In May 1977, she was pleased to join thirteen fellow GATC members to attend the ATC general meeting in Shepherdstown, West Virginia. Four members led workshops, and the club also presented a display with maps and photographs of their club activities. Their participation increased recognition within the Conference for the Georgia club's achievements at the same time that Georgia club members gained a perspective of the Trail project beyond the Georgia borders. Margaret was among those Georgia club members who were beginning to grasp the potential depth and breadth of the work of the ATC. And, the more she learned about the Appalachian Trail project beyond the Georgia borders, the more excited and engaged she became.

Margaret readily admitted that attending that meeting in West Virginia was an eye-opening experience for her. Through her participation in the workshops, meetings, and activities offered at the conference, she became increasingly aware of the issues facing the Appalachian Trail community. Land acquisitions, state's rights, federal appropriations, environmental regulations, and legal challenges all blended together into the broader responsibilities of the ATC. In addition, Margaret discovered that the other A.T. maintaining clubs were facing issues and meeting challenges that were very similar to her Georgia club.

Reflecting on the experience, Margaret stated, "We are sheltered having the Georgia Trail in the national forest." She was beginning to understand that this was not the case in other states where private property rights threatened the Trail. Margaret's comment about the Georgia Trail implies her growing awareness of the magnitude of the Appalachian Trail project, the importance of Trail-friendly government agencies such as the USDA Forest Service to the success of the project, and the vital role of volunteers who work tirelessly to gain the support of private landowners.

Indeed, the complexities of managing this Trail from Maine to Georgia were beginning to pique her interests. Just as Jean Stephenson's experiences in the Maine woods drew her well beyond the borders of the Potomac club, Margaret's experiences in West Virginia began to draw her far beyond the borders of the Georgia club.

Margaret's experiences at the 1977 conference in West Virginia also inspired her to grow the Georgia club into a model maintaining club. She returned to Atlanta with a greater understanding of her club's role in the Appalachian Trail project and with an increased commitment to Trail maintenance. For Margaret, a well-maintained trail was a great source of pride, and so she naturally championed the role of volunteer trail maintainers. The GATC board echoed her stance on Trail maintenance by providing extra incentives to club members who participated in work trips. Whether through board incentives or Margaret's welcoming "do as I do" attitude, the year 1977 was remembered for being the year in which two work trips were scheduled and twelve were actually held. Then, at the club's annual meeting, Margaret announced a new club award, "Trail Worker of the Year," further promoting trail maintenance as a core function of the Georgia club. That annual recognition was to be given to a GATC member who had been an outstanding worker on the Trail and for the club during the previous year. Lymen Emerson was honored with the first

"Trail Worker of the Year" award, and three other members received a "Trail Worker" patch.

Margaret's other priority as president was to engage the club membership in efforts to preserve the wilderness surrounding the Trail. She promoted the GATC's involvement in several broad initiatives, such as the Southern Appalachian Highlands Conservancy and the federal government's second Roadless Area Review & Evaluation (RARE II). Both projects were concerned with the official designation of lands — often adjacent to the A.T. — as wilderness areas. Under the direction of President Jimmy Carter, the RARE II was mandated to be carried out by the Forest Service. The study's objective was to identify roadless areas in the eastern United States that were on federal lands and consider them for official wilderness designation. Georgia club members attended workshops and submitted maps and information to the Forest Service. As a result of that work, Margaret reported in the December 1977 bulletin that most of the lands through which the Trail passed in Georgia met the necessary roadless criteria and were included in the final inventory. Although, in the end, the Forest Service's report became very controversial, especially with private landowners within the proposed wilderness areas, the Georgia club's involvement in the project focused its membership on the importance of protecting the wilderness areas surrounding the Trail. Today, the Trail passes through or along the edges of more than twenty-eight designated wilderness areas.

Finally, with board approval, albeit with dire predictions of failure from some board members, Margaret boldly requested that the club's 1978 schedule include one Trail maintenance work trip per month. Club records reveal that Margaret's ambitious goal did not meet with the anticipated failure. On the contrary, nearly one hundred members and guests participated in at least one work trip in 1978, with an average of seventeen people per trip and a total of almost 1,900 person-hours spent on Trail work during that year. Having shown only a mild interest in hiking when she first joined the Georgia club in 1961, Margaret was now clearly committed to lugging weed-trimmers, chain saws, and other heavy tools up mountains to install erosion bars, cut downed trees, and move rocks. As club president, her priority was to instill this same commitment in her fellow club members. As she prepared for her second year as club president, Margaret demonstrated a readiness to lead the GATC in maintaining the Appalachian Trail in Georgia with professionalism and enthusiasm. And, she was succeeding.

Welcoming new members into the Georgia club became a hallmark of Margaret's second year as club president. Margaret settled right in to build the club membership with her "just-come-join-us" attitude. But, unlike her predecessor Jim Coogler, Margaret did more than invite — she also mentored. According to fellow hikers, Margaret was a master at welcoming newcomers to join club hikes and then shepherding them onto committees or engaging them in projects. Several women within the Georgia club soon fell under her influence, and, perhaps unintentionally, Margaret became a role model for those women.

The Georgia club, as with many other A.T. maintaining clubs, had a long history of including, recognizing, and even celebrating the participation of women in all club activities. As early as 1933, four women found a place in Georgia club history as the FFFs, or Four Foolish Females. Marene Snow, Cynthia Ward, Olivia Herren, and Grace Ficken established a friendship that would endure for fifty years and exemplify the true spirit of the GATC.

As with the Potomac Appalachian Club, the Georgia club struggled in its early years with keeping a balance in its membership of men and women. In fact, the minutes of the June 1937 club council minutes included a reminder from member Arthur Stokes that the club constitution included the provision that membership be kept at approximately an equal balance of men and women, which was not being followed.

Ironically, the council agreed at this meeting that invitations to join the club would be extended to more masculine guests only to follow this decision with the election of Cynthia Ward in November as the club's first female president. Two years later, Marene Snow joined the council as historian, a position she held for twenty-four years. Just as Margaret embraced and then exceeded her label of "harried hike leader," these Georgia women embraced their reputation as the FFFs and then launched their own leadership positions within the GATC.

During Margaret's tenure as president, the increasing club membership reflected a well-balanced blend of men and women, who as hikers met the challenges of all types of weather and as Trail maintainers found satisfaction in hard, physical Trail work. One such woman was Rosalind Van Landingham, who, like Margaret, began her service on the GATC board of directors as bulletin editor. Roz, a native Georgian with a true affinity for anything outdoors, earned her undergraduate degree in biology from Birmingham Southern and a master's degree in zoology from Massachusetts' Smith College. Following graduation, Roz entered the Peace Corps and spent two years in India. Upon her return to the Atlanta area, she went to work for the Centers for Disease Control doing research in leprosy. Her career led her to Phoenix, Arizona, for several years, but, much like Margaret, she returned to make Atlanta her permanent home.

Roz's Trail career in many ways mimicked Margaret's: bulletin editor in 1978 and 1979, vice president in 1980, and then president in 1981 and 1982. Her service on the GATC board of directors would continue long after her presidency, with service as director-at-large during the years 1983–1985, conservation director in 1986-1987, information and education director in 1988–1989, and director-at-large again in 1990.

Somewhat unlike Margaret, Roz displayed much hardier outdoor interests, such as leading winter backpacking trips and challenging treks, such as a seven-day, one-hundred-mile hike from Damascus, Virginia, to Erwin, Tennessee. Fellow club members described Roz as "a strong hiker with unsurpassed endurance, an effective and willing leader." And, in turn, Roz recalled many of her early hikes with the club. Margaret would often volunteer to drive. Roz recalls hopping into Margaret's car, where she was always made to feel welcome.

Other Georgia club women serving in leadership positions within the GATC during Margaret's presidency and demonstrating strong hiking skills were Marianne Skeen, Nancy Shofner, Shirley Dempsey, and Grace Rogers. Of those, Marianne followed most closely in Margaret's footsteps. She credits Margaret with encouraging her to expand her interests beyond her favorite activity of backpacking and into such areas as Trail maintenance and club governance. Marianne recalls Margaret constantly urging her to attend the GATC board meetings and ATC conferences with the words, "Just come on." As Marianne states, "So I came, and, as a result, became more active in the Georgia club and then also in ATC."

Margaret's open invitation to try new things and get more involved netted results, as Marianne went on to serve the Georgia club as trails supervisor in 1983 and 1984, then vice president in 1985 and 1986, and finally president in 1986 and 1987. Her service also included twelve years on ATC's board of managers, six of them as southern vice chair — an involvement inspired by her friend and mentor, Margaret Drummond.

In the club's 1978 yearbook, Margaret offered insights into what she understood to be the challenges facing the Georgia club. First, she placed priority on protection of the Trail corridor, and she called attention to national events that included Congress' anticipated authorization of $90 million (in 1978 dollars) for land acquisition to secure the corridor. Second, Margaret asserted her belief that the paramount role of the individual clubs was to maintain the Appalachian Trail. According to Margaret, the role of the volunteer maintainers could only be safeguarded through a concerted effort to professionalize the methods by which they performed Trail maintenance. Shrugging that basic responsibility, she believed, would undermine and jeopardize the role of the clubs in the Trail project.

With this warning, Margaret set a course to standardize the methods by which the GATC maintained the Trail and to strengthen its connection to the ATC. Her enthusiasm to meet these challenges — while not always echoed by some of the independent-minded Georgia club maintainers — is obvious as she stated, "At the national level, the picture is exciting…. At the local level, Trail protection, *i.e.,* Trail maintenance, will be needed as never before."

Indeed, it was an exciting time for the Appalachian Trail. On March 21, 1978, President Jimmy Carter signed amendments to the National Trails System Act authorizing $90 million for the acquisition of lands along the A.T. With the express purpose of rallying the maintaining clubs, the May/June edition of ATC's *Appalachian Trailway News* included these comments from Margaret on the significance of this historic federal funding:

> It appears that volunteers may be asked for greater involvement in Trail maintenance, a challenge which the GATC enthusiastically accepts. There may be a greater need for organization of Trail management at the Conference and the Club levels….

Margaret's insistent promotion of Trail maintenance within the Georgia club dovetailed perfectly with the position of the Appalachian Trail Conference's board of managers during this turning point in A.T. history. She was the right person, in the right position, at the right time.

Since Lyndon Johnson's signing of the National Trails System Act in 1968, the Appalachian Trail enjoyed its designation as a national park, but until the 1978 funds authorization, the designation offered little real protection of the corridor. The amendment, referred to as "The Appalachian Trail Bill," was a windfall for the A.T. project. ATC and the A.T. National Park Office could now step up efforts to purchase land and easements to secure a continuous corridor from Maine to Georgia. The 1978 authorization mandated federal action to purchase lands adjacent to the Trail, giving relief to those who predicted that the Trail was destined to lose its wilderness qualities.

But, most important for the Conference and its maintaining clubs, the Appalachian Trail bill officially and explicitly recognized volunteer Trail maintainers as vital partners in the management of the A.T. As ATC's board chairman George Zoebelein wrote, "This new legislation is probably the most significant bill affecting the Trail project since its inception. Its passage means a new relationship with A.T. volunteers in order to maintain a footpath whose corridor will be owned by federal and state agencies."

President Carter's signing of the bill marked the formal, official beginning of what many refer to as "the era of cooperative management" in the A.T. project, although ATC and the two major federal agencies involved had had two- and three-way agreements since the 1930s and Dave Richie had been developing a cooperative-management model for the A.T. since becoming involved in 1976.

Under the 1978 bill, the Conference and its maintaining clubs now found themselves in the federal limelight. The bill and its authorization of funds placed newfound attention on the maintaining clubs and their volunteer trail maintainers to demonstrate their ability to maintain the Trail or risk "governmentalizing" the Trail project.

As Zoebelein warned, "The A.T. tradition [of volunteerism] must not be allowed to erode." Heeding that warning, the board of managers and its small staff reacted by concentrating efforts on solidifying relationships with the Trail-maintaining clubs and urging them to professionalize their maintenance of the Trail. The clubs had to raise standards for trail maintenance or risk a possible government take-over of this traditional volunteer role.

The $90-million authorization, which eventually grew to more than $200 million in appropriations by early in this century, brought with it the need for

ATC and its Trail-maintaining clubs to establish credibility with the federal agencies involved in the management of the Trail — led by the National Park Service and the USDA Forest Service. Margaret, at the helm of the Georgia club, was ready and excited to accept those challenges.

However, the road forward was not easy. As the Conference's board of managers focused efforts on professionalizing the volunteer work of its clubs, some pushback occurred. Well-seasoned Trail maintainers expressed disapproval with what they viewed as government interference in their long-established volunteer work, and such attitudes occasionally led to tensions between the maintaining clubs and the Conference.

In contrast, Margaret was credited with steering the Georgia club into accepting the directives being offered by the Conference. As someone who had experienced first-hand the pride that Trail workers felt at the end of a hard day on the Trail, Margaret understood the importance of fostering a mutually respectful relationship with ATC and the federal agencies. Her goal was to bring mutual respect into the three-way partnership of her club, ATC, and the federal government.

Margaret was unabashed in pledging her club's commitment to Trail maintenance. Later in the spring of 1978, when ATC Executive Director Hank Lautz visited the Georgia club, Margaret led her board of directors to unanimously vote to increase its responsibility for Trail maintenance. Margaret then turned to the general membership and requested that each member attend at least one work trip during 1978.

Although that goal was not realized, the club finished the year with nearly one hundred members and guests participating in Trail maintenance — a remarkable accomplishment.

A leader in university and faculty endeavors as well as in women's and environmental activities, Dr. Margaret Drummond sets a pace that few can follow.

From Emory University's "Campus Report," October 30, 1978

DR. MARGARET DRUMMOND

Often described as "a soft-spoken gentlewoman" with a distinct aversion for speaking about herself, Margaret was one to insist that her friends within the A.T. community "just call me Margaret." In fact, many within her growing circle of Trail friends knew little about her career as a professor of microbiology and lecturer at Atlanta's Emory University.

The October 30, 1978, issue of the university's biweekly newsletter, "The Campus Report," provided a rare glimpse into the academic life of Dr. Margaret Drummond. In this brief article, the spotlight was on Margaret as chair of the university senate and member of the women's caucus and the president's commission on the status of women. She also was recognized as recipient of several grants to study *staphylococcal coagulase* — a subject well beyond her better-known Trail world. In addition to recognizing her current work teaching microbiology to medical, nursing, dental, and allied-health students, the article focused on Margaret's efforts to raise the university's awareness of the plight of its women faculty members. As Dr. Drummond, she clearly stated, "I don't consider myself an activist."

Nevertheless, in the mid-1970s, Margaret helped to organize "brown-bag" luncheon meetings for the few women faculty members at Emory to discuss common challenges. In a 1995 interview with Judy Jenner, Margaret recalled that the group was not very effective in the beginning, but it soon attracted eighteen to twenty women on the faculty and a few administrative officials who were women. Over time, this loosely organized group evolved into a formal women's caucus with a campus-wide voice that spoke out on a number of issues facing university women.

Having earned tenure and full professorship, Margaret was in a more secure position than other women faculty to become embroiled in women's issues on campus, although she stated in the 1995 interview, "I was late to women's causes. I was of the generation that did what men said and never questioned authority."

The issue of women's equality in the workplace did not hit America's university scene until the mid-1960s, but its roots go back to a labor law that was first introduced in 1935 under the title, "Affirmative Action." Originally intended to encourage workers who believed they had been discriminated against by their employer to take an "affirmative action," the law was in effect married with civil rights for African-Americans and then merged with women's rights under President Johnson and expanded under President Richard Nixon.

Margaret recalled that the level of consciousness for women's rights was raised throughout Emory when the university president formed an affirmative action committee to study the treatment of women members of the faculty and then thoughtlessly proceeded to select an all-male roster to serve on the committee. Margaret responded. She marched into the office of the president to point out this oversight, only to find herself being offered the position of chair for the new committee. Of course, she accepted.

That began six years of teamwork that concluded with the committee presenting an interim report on the status of women to the university's incoming president. Many of her fellow university faculty members — both women and men — considered this report to be high among Margaret's many achievements while at Emory.

The photograph that accompanied the 1978 article in the "Campus Report" spoke volumes about this remarkable woman. Here Margaret smiles casually, while wearing a white lab coat and being surrounded by file cabinets and specimens. In contrast, the article also recognized Margaret's life beyond the classroom, stating that she was frequently spotted around campus in hiking gear and accompanied by her two Weimaraner dogs, Freidi and Brun Hilda. In all, Margaret appeared as a woman who was quite "comfortable in her skin."

Whether in the classroom, lecture hall, or the committee room, she was portrayed as a thoroughly competent university woman. Her trail friends would be quick to add similar accolades for her competencies on the Trail.

Probably, the most notable of her accomplishments has been to focus our attention on our responsibilities for the protection and maintenance of the Trail.

The Georgia Mountaineer, December 1978

Clockwise from top left: Margaret in her early days at GATC; working on the Trail; unveiling a new Approach Trail plaque at Amicalola Falls State Park; and opening the new Toccoa River bridge in 1977 with Chattahoochee National Forest Supervisor Pat Thomas.

Clockwise from top left: Taking a break on a trip to Max Patch; on the Trail taking notes for her guidebook; presiding at the 1985 Southern Partnership Committee meeting.

Clockwise from top left: Margaret taking a break during another 1985 meeting; awaiting visitors at the Georgia A.T. club booth at a biennial meeting; following her last meeting as ATC chair, in 1995, with a copy of a congratulatory letter from President Bill Clinton; during a break in the 1994 club presidents' meeting with Vice Chairs Sara Davis and Bob Epps.

Top: With previous chairs, left to right, George Zoebelein, Ray Hunt, and Stan Murray. Above, working on that log for a shelter. Left, with National Park Service director Roger Kennedy, left, and NPS A.T. Superintendent John Byrne in 1994, preparing to sign a renewal of the landmark cooperative agreement between ATC and the agency.

Clockwise from top left: With Dave Field, her successor, at a Board of Managers meeting; reluctantly posing in 1995 for an "official" photograph; in 1991, preparing to sign historic-preservation easement documents for April Hill farm in Massachusetts with Charles Sloan, chair of the Trust for A.T. Lands advisory committee, and Mary-Margaret Sloan, owner of the property and longtime major ATC donor.

"C" IS FOR COOPERATION, COMMITMENT, COMMITTEES, AND CONSENSUS

In November 1978, Margaret took another major step toward improving and strengthening the relationship between what she fondly referred to as "my club" and ATC. She organized GATC's first trail skills workshop, invited representatives from government and nongovernmental agencies to serve as instructors, and carefully presented the project to her fellow club members. Proposed as a cooperative effort with ATC and the Georgia Forest Service, the trail skills workshop presented Margaret with just the opportunity that she wanted. Here was the chance to offer her club as the host of a pilot project that would hopefully evolve into a series of regional workshops to be offered to all maintaining clubs from Maine to Georgia. Here was the chance for her club to shine.

And so, Margaret set to work planning for the workshop. She joined forces with Rima Farmer, southern field representative for ATC, to secure the services of the Project Office's Bob Proudman (previously a longtime trail-management worker for the Appalachian Mountain Club and later ATC's trail-management director) to be the main instructor. ATC's associate director, Dave Startzell; the Smoky Mountain Hiking Club's Jim Botts; and representatives from the Forest Service and Georgia Department of Natural Resources also provided instruction.

With expert instructors in place, Margaret faced a looming challenge — how to avoid placing her club members in the role of students being taught by outsiders. Her university experiences helped her to realize that to do so could jeopardize the success of the workshop.

Margaret understood that key to the success of the trail skills workshop was to first affirm the ability of each seasoned maintainer and to then create a rationale and enthusiasm for standardizing their Trail-maintenance skills. Her own experience as a Trail maintainer taught her that seasoned Trail maintainers were an independent lot. They knew how to do their job — had been doing it for years. Introducing standards by which the Trail was to be maintained, instituting methods for reporting Trail conditions, and requiring new forms for tracking volunteer hours could easily be viewed as unwanted, outside interference. To avoid these perceptions, Margaret depended on her selected team of exceptionally talented and Trail-smart instructors to display sensitivity to sometimes rough, gruff, and hard-core Trail maintainers.

Also, in a deliberate effort to avoid a structured classroom climate, Margaret chose to plan the workshop as a hands-on experience. Her outside team of instructors would work side-by-side with Georgia club maintainers to scout, flag, and cut a relocation over Blood Mountain. By adopting that format for the workshop, Margaret wisely side-stepped the traditional roles of teacher and students. Then, as she began promoting the workshop, she used her trademark "everyone-is-welcome" attitude to ease the volunteer maintainers' apprehensions over outside control. In so doing, the workshop was promoted as an outdoor experience for local trail maintainers and a team of representatives from various agencies beyond the Georgia borders to share, learn, and practice Trail-maintaining techniques.

Following the weekend-long workshop, Margaret took to the club bulletin to report on the participants' accomplishments. Her enthusiasm was obvious, as she listed four major accomplishments: cutting a relocation, installing water bars, building rock cribbing, and learning the proper use of many specialized Trail-maintenance tools. Her words were filled with a sense of pride in the quality of Trail work accomplished by workshop participation and in the pure comradery that results from a job done well. Margaret was also bold enough to chide her fellow club members who did not attend the workshop with these words:

> A GATC member and former Trails supervisor remarked recently that Trail work is really pretty dull and routine, splashing paint and hacking weeds. That member should have attended the Club's first Trails Skills Workshop and seen the CAPACITY crowd of energetic participants scrambling all over the side of Blood Mountain.... What they LEARNED would take up more space than the Editor allows...but was in part a heightened self-confidence and sense of accomplishment. Lest you think the weekend was all work..., there was fun and fellowship during the overnight at Camp Glisson....

In that cooperative effort, the Georgia club came through with exceptional participation, increased skills, and true Trail friendship. The outside team gained a deeper understanding of the challenges faced by the local Georgia club maintainers, and those maintainers broadened their understanding of the challenges inherent in maintaining the Trail from Maine to Georgia. Most important, new friendships were made through the trail skills workshop — perhaps, for Margaret, that was the best measure of success.

Margaret welcomed the new knowledge and new friendships that resulted from the trail skills workshop, and she was committed to instilling those same attitudes in her fellow Georgia club members — those who participated in the workshop and those who did not. All during her presidency of the Georgia club, she worked toward that goal. As she commented in that May/June 1978 *Appalachian Trailway News*, "Whatever lies ahead, however, GATC is ready and eager to assume a leadership role in the project to which it has been committed for almost 50 years, the maintenance and preservation of the Appalachian Trail." With those words, Margaret was committing herself and her club to the tasks that lay ahead. Perhaps she was also beginning to see a role for herself beyond the Georgia borders. Margaret was proud of her club's growing commitment to maintain the A.T., and her sights were clearly focused upon "whatever lies ahead."

While the trail skills workshop was a new venture, two traditional activities of the Georgia club continued under Margaret's presidency: the multiclub meet and the annual walk-thru. In April, thirty-seven club members and guests participated in the fourth annual walk-thru, as the condition of the entire Trail in Georgia was checked and sections were scheduled for improvements. Then, on Labor Day weekend, eleven GATC members and friends joined with Margaret to represent the club at the annual multiclub meeting at Roan Mountain, Tennessee. Held each year since 1932, the multiclub meeting brought together the southern A.T. maintaining clubs to discuss common issues. According to Margaret's report in *The Georgia Mountaineer*, those attending the 1978 multiclub meeting also enjoyed superb weather, challenging hiking, incomparable fellowship, and ripe blueberries. Her words were clearly directed toward her fellow Georgia club members to become involved — as she was — in the broader Trail community.

Committee work was another hallmark of Margaret's years as GATC president. Several committees were exceptionally active under her leadership. For example, in 1978, the conservation committee prepared a position paper for the RARE II wilderness proposal. The education committee presented programs on hypothermia and backpacking. The maps committee prepared a ranking of the difficulty levels of the sections of the A.T. in Georgia and measured the Loop Trail at 35.5 miles long.

Fellow Georgia club members also credited Margaret with providing the leadership to bring disparate groups into the decision-making process and shepherding them to consensus. A prime example was Margaret's role in pushing for a long-awaited resolution of the proposed Georgia extension to the Blue Ridge Parkway. For decades, the GATC had grappled with this proposal and its likely effect on the A.T. in Georgia. The development of Skyline Drive in Virginia's Shenandoah National Park created an historic rift among the early founders of the A.T. project and a lingering suspicion that mountaintop parkways deprived the Trail of its wilderness qualities. Many members within the Georgia club, Margaret included, viewed an extension of the Blue Ridge Parkway as a similar threat.

GATC presidents before Margaret had long anguished over this issue as they sought to interpret federal actions that appeared contradictory. On one hand, the October 1968 signing of the National Trails System Act bestowed national park status upon the A.T., while the almost simultaneous passage of the Blue Ridge Parkway Extension bill heightened concerns that the A.T. in Georgia was in jeopardy.

In the years since 1968, the Georgia club sought assistance in opposing the parkway extension from a variety of state and national conservation groups, including The Nature Conservancy and The Wilderness Society. ATC's Jean Stephenson and A.T. founder Benton MacKaye also were consulted, with MacKaye offering his classic inspirational yet vague messages. In contrast, Jean — in her typical, methodical mindset — went to work studying topographic maps, drawing up plans for an alternate route for the parkway, and presenting it to parkway officials and engineers in Washington. As with all the efforts by the GATC, none of Jean's efforts brought the parkway issue closer to a resolution. Consequently, the Georgia club's response to date was to create a trail relocation committee charged with scouting and marking an alternate route for the Trail and then to wait for federal action.

This wait-and-watch strategy ended during Margaret's first year as GATC president, when she penned a letter to the A.T. Project Office of the National Park Service asking for a determination and expressing the club's desire to have the "old A.T." reinstated as the official route. As might be expected, her actions did not result in an immediate response. However, Margaret persisted in seeking a final resolution even after her two-year term as the GATC president ended. When *The Georgia Mountaineer* announced in February 1982 that the official A.T. in Georgia was to remain on the 50-year-old, white-blazed, ridgetop location, many long-time members of the Georgia club recalled Margaret's tenacity and perseverance. Finally, in March 1989, Blue Ridge Parkway Superintendent Gary E. Everhardt stated publicly that he was in favor of deauthorizing the parkway extension project and keeping the A.T. on the mountain ridge.

Although government deauthorization continued to languish as late as 1993, Margaret's leadership within the GATC that urged opposition to the extension proposal was a bold act that necessitated thoughtful and persistent communications among the Georgia club, the larger Conference, and federal government agencies. In this situation, as in many others, Margaret demonstrated her ability to build consensus and seek resolution without alienating those involved in the issue. As Rosalind Van Landingham noted in an interview, "Margaret repeatedly displayed her intelligence, a great sense of organization, and an ability to stimulate conversation." Those traits were beginning to meet with success, to the benefit of the A.T.

In December 1978, as the second and final year of Margaret's presidency came to a close, the GATC honored her at the club's annual Christmas party. The ceremony credited Margaret with renewing the GATC's commitment to trail maintenance. Incoming President Whit Benson presented Margaret with the first copy of the club's annual yearbook, featuring a picture of Margaret painting a blaze on a tree, and the framed original drawing from which the cover image was made. The drawing captured Margaret's dedication to trail maintenance and the enjoyment she received from trail work. Characterizing her as "a totally involved president," Whit offered words of praise for Margaret by stating, "[She] pursued her duties with her usual enthusiasm and careful attention to all areas of GATC activity…. We all say 'Thanks, you did a great job!'"

Largely due to Margaret's leadership, the Georgia club became a model Appalachian Trail-maintaining club with a membership that was proud of its partnership with ATC and the many government agencies involved in the Trail project. As described in *Friendships of the Trail: The History of the Georgia Ap-*

palachian Trail Club 1930-1980, "Her presidency seemed to be a turning point in the direction of the Club...toward a greater responsibility for the upkeep of the Trail.... None of the light-heartedness of former years was lost, but now the Trail-building activities were among the 'in' events." Throughout her presidency, Margaret often expressed pride in her club, and now, as her presidency came to an end, her club was proud of her.

During her two years as president of the GATC, Margaret seized many opportunities to hone her leadership skills within the Georgia Trail community. The challenges and successes she experienced — from harried hike leader to totally involved president — would prove valuable as her horizons expanded beyond Georgia to the larger Appalachian Trail community.

Even before her service as president of the GATC came to an end, Margaret was attracting the attention of the leadership within ATC as someone with exceptional skills. From comprehending complex issues, to forming and directing committees, promoting partnerships, and shepherding disparate groups toward consensus, this university woman had much to offer the Conference. And, fortunately for the Conference, Margaret was similarly attracted to the Trail challenges and opportunities that lay beyond her Georgia borders. She may have stepped down as the GATC president as 1978 came to a close, but she was *not* stepping out of the Appalachian Trail community.

> *Margaret was best at bringing people together and never acting in a hostile way, but I recall in a meeting to discuss the extension of the Blue Ridge Parkway into Georgia, Margaret stamped her foot on the floor with the simple words, "Leave my trail alone."*
>
> **Rosalind Van Landingham, Interview on January 8, 2018**

BALANCING TRAIL ACTIVITIES

In 1979, Margaret began a balancing act of continuing service to the GATC while increasing participation in the ATC and spearheading other trail projects. Although her term as president of GATC came to an end, she continued to serve as a director-at-large on the board of directors through 1981. She also continued to have a positive impact on the Georgia club in many other ways.

For example, as a direct result of the 1978 trail skills workshop, the club entered into a cooperative agreement with the Forest Service, and Chattahoochee National Forest Supervisor Pat Thomas agreed to the loan of maintenance tools to the club. Pat had stood with Margaret during the ceremony that opened the Toccoa River Bridge in November 1977, and Margaret — always the one to recognize the value of a partnership — had continued to cultivate that friendship. Although the loaning of tools was a small gesture of friendship, Margaret was able to demonstrate to her fellow club members the value of nurturing this partnership.

Also as a result of the trail skills workshop, the Forest Service began to realize that the Georgia club was willing and able to build and maintain the Trail. However, until new members could be recruited or other groups could be identified to help, the Forest Service also accepted the realization that the Georgia club would continue to be dependent and thankful for the assistance of the Forest Service.

In addition to her continued service as a director-at-large, Margaret chaired the GATC's conservation committee. Just one month after stepping down as president, she reported at the January 1979 board meeting that five areas in the state had been proposed for inclusion in the RARE II wilderness areas. Two of those areas were to include portions of the A.T. in Georgia. Concerns were immediately expressed as to whether the typical wilderness restrictions on the use of power tools and the building of shelters would apply in the event that these A.T. sections were ultimately designated as within wilderness areas. However, as to be expected, these concerns began to fade, when a decision by Congress on the wilderness issue became as elusive as the determination of an official A.T. route in Georgia.

In March 1979, Margaret assisted with yet another attempt to encourage the federal government to finally resolve the issue of official designation of the Appalachian Trail route through Georgia. To this end, Margaret rallied Georgia club members to flag the remote Chattahoochee Basin section of the Trail. The purpose was to allow for a comparison of the original white-blazed route and the reroute, and the objective was to push for a long overdue determination of which route would become the official, federally designated route of the A.T. through Georgia.

The March 3 work trip proved to be very difficult, with challenging terrain, poor weather, and the nagging thought that no amount of work would resolve the Trail location issue. Once again, Margaret penned an upbeat report of the day's work in *The Georgia Mountaineer*. She was also clear in the result: "The present ridgetop white-blazed Trail is the preferred route for the A.T. in Georgia, except for the short distance between Springer Mountain and the Cross Trails Shelter where the blue-blazed Trail is recommended." She was equally emphatic in her conclusion, "The Task Force hopes to lose no more time in the resolution of this thorny and now longtime problem of TWO A.T.'s in Georgia." Margaret wanted the federal government's indecision to end.

The 1979 GATC calendar indicated that a trail maintenance work trip was held every month with the exception of August, an accomplishment that earned Margaret's praise. Reports submitted by the work-trip leaders praised the diehards who refused to be defeated by snow and below-freezing temperatures on Blood Mountain that threatened the success of the January work crew and rain and fog that challenged the February crew. However, it was the club's involvement in ATC's biennial meeting that interfered with the scheduling of a work trip in August — an excuse that met with Margaret's approval. She boasted in the club bulletin of the many ways the Georgia club contributed to the ATC biennial meeting held August 10-14 in Maine, but she modestly left it to GATC's President Whit Benson to announce that the biennial meeting also included the election of Margaret to a position on the ATC board of managers.

Margaret was ready to embark on a much larger role within the A.T. community. She also was most likely quite pleased to see Rosalind Van Landingham step into the position of GATC's bulletin editor. Having served as editor since 1968, Margaret expressed both enthusiasm and confidence in the selection of her replacement. "Roz" was now ready to launch her own long-term commitment to the Georgia club, while Margaret was on her own trajectory.

Early in 1980, Margaret participated in meetings of the southern regional management committee and Appalachian National Scenic Trail Advisory Council (ANSTAC), where once again uncertainties continued for a deauthorization of the parkway bill and the designation of the official route of the A.T. through Georgia. While those federal issues remained in limbo, the Georgia club moved forward with work to establish the Benton MacKaye Trail (BMT).

Margaret became deeply involved in that project. Long recognized as the visionary for the Appalachian Trail, MacKaye maintained a special friendship with the Georgia club. To honor that friendship, the Georgia club had agreed in early 1980, at the request of Randy Snodgrass, president of the newly formed Benton MacKaye Trail Association (BMTA), to help establish that new trail. When completed, the BMT would form a large, figure-eight loop with the Appalachian Trail through Georgia, North Carolina, and Tennessee. GATC's side-trails committee, under the direction of Grant Wilkins, volunteered to flag the 60-mile section of the BMT in Georgia — all in one day, April 5, 1980.

On that day, GATC members and guests and BMTA members and guests divided up into small groups and fanned out over preplanned sections of the proposed trail route with compasses and topographical maps in hand, to flag the route. As a founding member of the BMTA, Margaret enthusiastically joined this initial effort. She later recalled, "We were really pioneers — starting something new. It captured everyone's imagination."

When the GATC board voted to relinquish its jurisdiction of the Loop Trail on Springer Mountain in order to further concentrate efforts on maintaining the A.T., the BMTA planned to locate its trail on a portion of the Loop Trail. The balance of the Loop Trail was subsequently converted to a national recreation trail under the supervision of the Forest Service.

Margaret now seemed to be in a perfect place — with the Georgia section of the Appalachian Trail to maintain, the Benton MacKaye Trail to build, and new friends to make within ATC. She enjoyed balancing these growing trail commitments with her teaching and research responsibilities at Emory. While one occupied her Monday through Friday work week, the other filled her weekends with the type of outdoor labor that she thoroughly enjoyed. For example, during this time, she regularly attended second-Saturday work trips on the Benton MacKaye Trail and third-Saturday work trips with the GATC. Those two trails were beginning to fill most of her leisure time.

Although an optimist, I am not a pollyanna."

Margaret Drummond's Message,
Appalachian Trailway News, March/April 1990

YES, WE CAN DO THIS!

Nineteen-eighty was the golden anniversary of the Georgia Appalachian Trail Club, so an anniversary committee was formed at the end of 1979 to plan special events that would occur throughout the year. While plans moved forward for a big 50th birthday party, the Appalachian Trail Conference was facing serious financial troubles. The Conference appealed to the then-thirty maintaining clubs to contribute $3 per club member to help weather that difficult time. A fellow member of the Georgia club, Marianne Skeen, credited Margaret with showing her fellow Georgia club members the "humanity side" of the larger ATC.

According to Marianne, Margaret projected a "yes, we can do this" attitude capable of neutralizing the tensions that could easily materialize between the local clubs and the broader Conference when faced with an appeal to provide financial assistance. Margaret, being in her second year as a director-at-large for the GATC and also serving on the board of managers for ATC, felt a responsibility to respond to the needs of both organizations.

Rather than dwelling on the reasons behind ATC's financial woes, Margaret proposed to hold a flea market in the front yard of GATC club member Jennifer Harvey. The GATC board agreed to raise the funds through this special project, and club members supported her idea by donating camping and household items. The event was an amazing success — netting more than $1,000, $650 of which was sent to ATC. Margaret found a way for GATC to respond to the financial needs of ATC, while not impacting its own treasury, but rather involving club members in an enjoyable activity that, in turn, fostered goodwill and strengthened relations with the Conference — a "win" for all.

Other activities in 1980 included the traditional multiclub meeting, hosted that year by the GATC. The event proved once again that, when the Georgia club members get behind an event, it will turn into a huge success. Every GATC committee got involved in the multiclub meeting: history, education, and trails information committees prepared a historical display; the photographic committee presented a slide show. Other club members offered hiking seminars, hikes, and a campfire program. Margaret served as the ATC liaison during the planning of the event, which attracted 150 members representing all of the southern clubs.

The year closed with GATC's big event in December celebrating the 50th anniversary of its founding. Preparations included locating and inviting nearly one hundred former members, among them Cynthia Ward Muise, the first woman president of the club, and Elizabeth White, the longest-standing club member, having joined in 1930 only days after its organization. Pioneer member Marene Snow blew out the candles atop a beautiful cake created by club Vice President Rosalind Van Landingham. Friendships old and new were celebrated with a square dance, displays, decorations, and a slide show of photographs from the 1930s.

Nineteen-eighty ended on an exceptionally high note due to the success of that celebration, as stated in the club's *Friendships of the Trail:* "The Club has a dogged determination to shape the Georgia portion of the Trail as it sees it — come hell, high water, the Forest Service, conference, or whoever. We fought for this Trail; we built it with our sweat, blisters, and laughter; and we're immensely proud of it." As the Georgia club members looked optimistically forward to the next fifty years of Trail friendships, Margaret was similarly focused on her expanding, exciting, and new roles within the Trail project.

The following year, Rosalind Van Landingham stepped into the presidency of the GATC and reasserted Margaret's commitment to the maintenance of the A.T. in Georgia. Club members responded by joining work trips in ever-increasing numbers. Margaret had surely set the club on a course of fulfilling its responsibility for maintaining the Trail with a spirited sense of comradery. This dedication with comradery was evident during the club's March 22-23 overnight maintenance trip, when Margaret and twenty-three fellow energetic workers logged 185 person-hours of Trail maintenance. While not entirely ignoring everyone's sore muscles and heavy eyes, Margaret insisted that her fellow workers spend some of their evening hours writing letters to elected officials asking for their support to oppose President Reagan's plan to rescind the 1981 fiscal year's appropriation of funds for land acquisition along the A.T.

Friendships within the Georgia club were strong, and so those tired Trail workers conceded to Margaret's wishes. The letters were written as requested. Margaret would continue throughout the coming years to further engage the GATC members in the broader issues of the Conference. As a result, her fellow

Georgia club members would begin thinking beyond the Georgia borders of the Trail, and eventually several followed her into leadership roles within the Conference.

During 1982, financial woes continued to plague the Conference, and Margaret continued to rally for the GATC to offer assistance. When the Georgia club's board of directors voted to contribute $1 for each of its current members, Margaret published the decision in the club's April bulletin, once again proudly congratulating her club for setting an example that would encourage other maintaining clubs to do their part to ease the Conference's financial situation.

She followed up in May with a report to GATC on another issue facing the Conference: timber harvesting. Apparently, a consortium of the New England clubs had requested permission to harvest timber within the corridor purchased by the Appalachian Trail Project Office and return the proceeds to the clubs for Trail-maintenance expenses. As a member of ATC's board of managers, Margaret was able to offer a full report of this issue to the Georgia club, and her report may have led the GATC board to vote unanimously to oppose timber harvesting on A.T. acquired lands. Ironically, Margaret later became part of the Conference's decision to defer ruling on the timber-harvesting issue until other regions could respond.

Perhaps to balance such serious issues, the Georgia club offered its hardiest members a new event in 1982. Designed to foster friendships while testing the endurance of hikers, the event was the first marathon day-hike of the A.T. in Georgia. The rules were simple. Hikers were to begin at the A.T.'s southern terminus on Springer Mountain at 7:30 a.m. on May 15 and go as far as they liked. Although Margaret was not likely to engage in this type of event, her fellow women hikers relished the challenge. Whit Benson finished first, covering thirty-three miles in twelve hours and twenty minutes. Nancy Shofner, Marianne Skeen, and Roz Van Landingham finished directly on his heels. Roz, true to her reputation for endurance, followed this event with a seven-day, 100-plus-mile hike on the A.T. in Virginia and Tennessee!

Margaret again took to pen and paper to report in the July 1982 issue of the Georgia club bulletin on a project close to her heart: the Benton MacKaye Trail. As a founding member of this fledgling trail association, Margaret spelled out the accomplishments over the past two years: fifteen miles constructed, twenty miles of the former Loop Trail cleared and reblazed as the BMT, and additional route selections beginning in North Carolina and Tennessee.

In addition to reporting on these accomplishments, Margaret submitted another report that included the announcement that the GATC had become the first of the A.T. maintaining clubs to reach the goal of having one hundred percent of its Trail protected, all within Forest Service lands. This announcement proved to be a bit premature, as the final parcel would not be acquired for several years.

Nonetheless, 1982 was a year of well-deserved recognition for Margaret's Trail work. An article in the September 1982 club bulletin announced that Margaret had received special recognition from Georgia's Governor George Busbee, and she was also appointed by Interior Secretary James Watts to be a new state representative to the Appalachian National Scenic Trail Advisory Council (ANSTAC), a key institution in the 1980s in bringing together the federal agencies, the states, and all the private organizations involved with the A.T. as a cooperative network. Margaret continued to serve on that council until it was disbanded in 1988 under a sunset provision in the law. Throughout that time, she also continued as field editor of several editions of the *Appalachian Trail Guide to North Carolina-Georgia,* spanning the period 1970 to 1985.

As noted, Margaret's growing service to ATC did not diminish her dedication to the Georgia club. When President Rosalind Van Landingham asked for a review of the club's long tradition of requiring two sponsors in order to be considered for membership, Margaret, as membership director, responded. In September 1982, she provided a full report to GATC's board of directors. Her findings concluded that the requirement that prospective members be sponsored into the club by two current members should be continued, but all other requirements for sponsorship should be dropped. This meant an end to stipulations that sponsors must hike with the prospective member and that the two sponsors cannot be related. In striking a middle ground, Margaret's report also recommended that the current point system be retained, requiring fifteen points be earned by a prospective member in one year, three of which were to be earned through Trail maintenance. As a testament to Margaret's ability to keep the club's membership on a steady, solid path of growth and retain focus on Trail maintenance, the board approved each of these recommendations.

Margaret's thoughtful review followed by board action appeared to put the club on the right path, as club membership continued to rise from 250 in 1983 to 450 by 1990, and maintenance hours reached a decade high of nearly 5,000 hours in 1988. Obviously, the club was attracting members ready and willing to fulfill its founding mission of maintaining the Appalachian Trail in Georgia.

...to get people out of their own club group and to mingle to talk to each other,,,, This should become a tradition!

Margaret Drummond letter to Jim Botts, September 14, 1984

GAINING A NATIONAL PERSPECTIVE

In 1983, Margaret became a vice chair of the ATC, representing the southern region. In that position, she gained a national perspective of the Appalachian Trail project and reported regularly to the Georgia club on issues facing the Conference on the national level. She continued to participate in GATC's work trips, and her enthusiasm for Trail maintenance continued to spread to other members of the Georgia club. After having led Trail-maintenance work trips in May 1981 and 1982, Margaret willingly volunteered to lead another trail skills workshop in May 1983, with the same remarkable success as the first workshop held in 1978. This time, thirty enthusiastic club members under the direction of trails supervisor Marianne Skeen logged 165 hours of Trail work.

The 1980s were filled with many changes for GATC, ATC, and Margaret. Membership in the GATC grew at an astonishing rate, nearly doubling. In response to the 1984 signing of the A.T. delegation agreement by the National Park Service (NPS) and the Appalachian Trail Conference, the conference slowly expanded its central staff in Harpers Ferry and reinforced three and then four regional offices. ATC also began a long tradition in 1985 with the hosting of the first presidents' meeting, designed to bring together the presidents of all the A.T. maintaining clubs to discuss issues of common interest and establish open communications among them.

Margaret, then serving as a member of the ATC board of managers and vice chair of its southern region, was credited as instrumental in beginning presidents' meetings as a way of strengthening relationships among the clubs. GATC President Joe Boyd represented the Georgia club at this first meeting, which was held in conjunction with the ATC April board of managers meeting in Harpers Ferry. The 1986 presidents' meeting was likewise held in Harpers Ferry, and this time was attended by representatives of all thirty-one clubs. At the conclusion of that second presidents' meeting, it was announced that future meetings would be held every two years, to alternate with the biennial meetings. (ATC no longer hosts in-person biennial meetings, shifting to annual on-line meetings. It does seek funding in even-numbered years for what are now termed volunteer leadership meetings.)

Just as the 1980s posed many changes for the Conference, Margaret was also riding a wave of change. In the year following her retirement from Emory University's School of Medicine in 1988, Margaret stepped into the position of chair of ATC, a position she would hold for the maximum six years.

When Margaret assumed the chairmanship of the ATC in 1989, she understood well the long history of partnerships that sustained the organization. Three specific events in the evolution of the ATC demonstrate the power of partnerships. First, its very formation on March 3, 1925, when the Federated Society of Planning and Parks convened a meeting in Washington and succeeded in stitching together an executive committee of notable conservationists, government officials, foresters, and other professionals. (See pages 16-17.)

The second landmark partnership event in ATC history occurred on October 2, 1968. On this date, President Johnson signed Public Law 90-543, the National Trails System Act. This act established two long-distance trails — the Appalachian Trail and the Pacific Crest Trail — as our nation's first national scenic trails. The act and its legislative history established specific roles for the departments of the interior and agriculture and the ATC to administer cooperatively the Appalachian Trail and acquire lands to protect it. In short, the act and 1978 "A.T. amendments" to it spelled out the partnerships that would sustain the Trail and provide for its long-term protection.

A third partnership-strengthening event occurred on January 26, 1984, when the National Park Service signed a new, major A.T. cooperative agreement. That document officially assigned to the Appalachian Trail Conference the responsibility for maintaining the Trail on NPS-acquired lands. Although the Conference, through its maintaining clubs, had been building, clearing, relocating, and improving the footpath and facilities such as shelters and bridges before and since its completion in 1937, that agreement formalized those responsibilities now that the underlying pathway was public property. In many ways, the act solidified the mission of the Appalachian Trail Conference.

As Margaret ended an outstanding academic career at Emory in 1988, she was well-schooled in those historic moments in the Trail project. She had a broad and deep Trail résumé founded on the three-legged partnership of volunteer maintaining clubs, the Appalachian Trail Conservancy, and the federal agencies. She had forged a reputation for the Georgia Appalachian Trail Club as a progressive and exceptionally capable Trail-maintaining club, and she had built a well-respected reputation for herself as a defender of the clubs' role in the Trail project. As Margaret moved into the position of chair of ATC in 1989, she possessed the confidence of a well-seasoned leader within the A.T. community, ready to guide the Conference through the next exciting period in its remarkable history.

> *[The only way the partnership will work is] by meetings, listening to each other, realizing and accepting each other's constraints, finding solutions, negotiating and compromising when necessary, accepting successes and occasional failures, and respecting each other.*
>
> — Margaret Drummond in *Appalachian Trailway News,*
> July/August 2000

LEADING THE APPALACHIAN TRAIL CONFERENCE

As chair of the Appalachian Trail Conference, Margaret informally was expected to author the chair's message that appeared in each issue of the Conference's magazine, *Appalachian Trailway News.* Editor Judy Jenner recalled being puzzled at Margaret's occasional reluctance to pen the article. Perhaps as a university woman, Margaret held herself to a high standard of authorship that made the bimonthly task a chore. Nevertheless, in those articles, Margaret revealed much about herself, her beliefs, and her values. Perhaps it was this personal exposure that created her reluctance to author the articles. Within these articles, we also learn much about how she views her role as chair of ATC. Here Margaret outlined her intentions to delegate responsibilities to committees, promote partnerships, concentrate on the larger issues, develop strategies for conflict resolution, and support change — all skills that she developed at Emory and honed at the Georgia club.

Margaret often referred to herself as "an avowed committee advocate," a fact that is further explained in her November/December 1989 chair's message, where she characterized herself as coming from "a university background where much of the business is done in committees." She concluded this message by explaining that it took her more than two months to reconstitute ATC's committees for 1989-1991, because the board was now functioning with more than fifteen committees.

Regardless of her increased responsibilities as chair of ATC, Margaret continued to keep active with her Georgia club. Beginning in 1989, she was one of the instigators of GATC's Tuesday Hikers. When Margaret and Vivian and Lyman Emerson casually asked people to join them for a midweek hike, they were most likely very surprised to see their small group grow over time. First announced in GATC's January bulletin as the formation of the "Terrible Tuesday Hiking Group," this informal and unofficial club activity attracted sufficient hikers in its first month to necessitate the printing of a schedule in the February newsletter showing times and meeting places for all hikes to be held in the first quarter of the year. Even into 2005, GATC's midweek hikes were attracting up to forty participants.

Acknowledging the many management partners of the A.T. also became a key point of Margaret's bimonthly messages. In the March/April 1990 issue, she described a 1989 ATC event that attracted more than one hundred people representing "the full spectrum of A.T. management partners." In successive articles, she offers accolades to the thirty-one maintaining clubs, the National Park Service, and the Forest Service for their hard work. For example, the May/June 1993 message was titled, "Uniquely A.T.: People and Partnerships." When she was elected to another two-year term as chair of ATC in July 1993, she titled her July/August message, "More on A.T. Partnerships." When the cooperative agreement between ATC and the National Park Service was coming

up for renewal during 1993, Margaret concentrated her messages on informing the membership of the process and expressing optimism for the success of
this partnership. She signed off her November/December message with these
words, "I'll lose my credibility if I use the word 'partnership' another time."

Most likely, partnerships were much on her mind throughout 1993 as
the Georgia club joined with the Nantahala Hiking Club, Carolina Hiking
Club, Smoky Mountains Hiking Club, and the Tennessee Eastman Hiking
Club to host Deep South '93, the ATC biennial meeting. This was a major
undertaking, raising serious concerns within the ranks of the Georgia club
and not receiving unanimous support of the GATC board of directors. Margaret's longtime friend in the Georgia club, Marianne Skeen, agreed to chair
the steering committee, which would select the conference site, establish a budget, and organize a planning committee. Margaret reflected on the success
of the event in her September/October message titled, "Sharing their energy,
diversity." Here she celebrates the dedication shared by the maintaining clubs
despite their differences in membership size, length of Trail each stewards, and
the state and federal agencies setting policies within their geographic districts.
Margaret sums up the key to success in the Trail's management system in her
simple conclusion, "Communication is basic."

During the years 1994 and 1995, Margaret directed attention to the issue of securing ownership of the lands through which the Trail passed. The
September/October 1994 chair's message was entitled "Challenges to the footpath." Here, Margaret penned her message to the membership on the issues
surrounding a proposed ski resort on Saddleback Mountain, a high-intensity
power-line in Roanoke, Virginia, and a highway project on the Tennessee–
North Carolina border. Each posed serious threats to the Trail, its surrounding
greenway, and its expansive viewsheds. Margaret has been long remembered
for her concluding remark: "For a satisfactory resolution of those conflicts, we
need the wisdom of Solomon and the patience of Job."

One can easily imagine Margaret reflecting upon earlier experiences while
president of GATC, such as her repetitive efforts to end the Blue Ridge Parkway Extension project and, once and for all, to designate the original white-
blazed Trail as the official A.T. in Georgia. Margaret long understood that
thwarting projects that affected the A.T. demanded perseverance and patience,
and, she would add, "a common belief that the experience of a primitive Trail is

an experience worth preserving." That comment harkens back to many similar remarks made by A.T. visionary Benton MacKaye decades earlier.

Margaret was also clear in her messages of success, as in the November/ December 1994 chair's message entitled, "Trail Protection: Two Celebrations." Margaret hailed — a bit prematurely — a landmark achievement in A.T. history with her words, "The Trail footpath has been protected, *i.e.,* the permanent treadway is held in federal or state ownership."

During Margaret's tenure as ATC chair, federal appropriations for land acquisition made it possible to secure ninety-five percent of the treadway by placing lands along the Trail in public ownership. Margaret was able to look to the Georgia club with special pride as the entire section of the A.T. in that state was now protected through public land purchases, and she continued in her efforts to complete the land-acquisition process along the entire A.T. Her March/April 1995 message realistically concluded, "44 miles to go — so close." Continuing to keep her focus on the larger issue, she persisted in the article to implore the membership to write to their members of Congress, invite them on hikes, and encourage them to support federal appropriation of funds to complete the land-acquisition process.

When Margaret stepped down as chair in 1995, the Conference was continuing a process of long-range strategic planning she had instigated that would lead, over the next ten years, to a major reorganization of the Conference. The process would also result in changes for its maintaining clubs, opening the possibilities for contention and resistance. Margaret, as chair emeritus with a seat and vote on the board at the time, was in a position to help smooth the transition and argued eloquently against any measures that would diminish the roles of clubs and volunteers generally.

In the end, however, she was not present for the votes that changed the organization's name to Appalachian Trail Conservancy and adopted a corporate logo alongside the long-dominant Trail-marker "diamond."

Leader. Visionary. Forthright. Organized. Analytical. Friendly. Consensus-builder.

Shelley Rose describing Margaret Drummond
in the November 2005 issue of *The Georgia Mountaineer*

Awards & Recognitions

The first of a series of awards recognizing Margaret's contribution to the A.T. community came in 1992 when she received GATC's highest honor, the Friend of the Trail Award. The award recognizes individuals who have been GATC members for twenty-five years or more and who have made significant contributions to the Georgia club and the Appalachian Trail community. Margaret graciously received the award, which carries a lifetime membership in the GATC, at the club's annual holiday party.

Then in July 1995, Margaret's longtime friend Marianne Skeen presented Margaret with the coveted "image pin" from the southern region of the USDA Forest Service recognizing her exemplary volunteer service. The presentation was made during the ATC membership meeting in Harrisonburg, Virginia, and acknowledged Margaret's 34-year tenure as a volunteer on the Forest Service/A.T. Project. This was a very special moment for both women. Marianne, a fellow GATC member who was now serving on ATC's board of managers, was especially honored to make this presentation to the woman who had for so long inspired her to volunteer service in the A.T. project. The smiles that were exchanged as Marianne placed the pin on Margaret's shirt collar clearly expressed their mutual pleasure for a job well done and an award well deserved!

As outgoing ATC chair, Margaret was also honored at the general meeting when Executive Director David Startzell surprised her with a commendation from President Bill Clinton. In his letter, President Clinton states, "Your consistent efforts on the Conference Board have directly contributed to the advancement of one of America's greatest national treasures. You have served to ensure the Trail's continued maintenance, and your leadership has helped to give our national park system a brighter future."

As she began her new role as a chair emeritus of ATC, Margaret prepared to do what she described as "what 'normal' people do when they retire.... Gardening, reading, working with an investment club she and friends started." She also looked forward to spending more time with her companion and housemate, a three-year-old, 75-pound Weimaraner named Liesl.

More awards soon followed. In 1996, Margaret received the Chief's Award from the USDA Forest Service. As one of the few nonagency recipients of this award, Margaret was recognized for her assistance in acquiring significant tracts of land along the Trail through particularly difficult negotiations. The ceremony included presenting Margaret with a special plaque that Margaret described as "absolutely magnificent" and "as a gesture of recognition and affection from my longtime friends in the Forest Service."

In an exchange of letters following the award ceremony, Margaret once again found it necessary to acknowledge partnerships and volunteers who she considered to be at the heart of the A.T. project. She states, "I was honored to be singled out for recognition, but you must know partnerships such as ours here in Georgia have evolved through the work of hundreds (thousands?) of dedicated people over many years." Perhaps to gain the last words and set the record straight that Margaret, and Margaret alone, was deserving of this award, Bob Bolz of the Georgia Department of Natural Resources penned a letter to Margaret in June 1996 that included this statement, "Your magnanimous commitment to your fellow man, the environment, and especially to the Appalachian Trail are outstanding.... I consider it an honor to know you and to have had the opportunity to see you in action."

Then on August 2, 1997, at ATC's biennial meeting in Bethel, Maine, Margaret was designated an honorary member of ATC, the Conference's only official award for "service performed [that has] had an inspirational or exemplary effect because of its special quality/character or innovative aspects, rather than service of conventional nature but performed in a superior manner." Once again, Marianne Skeen, whom Margaret had mentored to become involved in Trail governance, had some words to share with fellow GATC members in *The Georgia Mountaineer.*"Her greatest legacy may be the new generations of volunteers whose confidence she has helped to build by offering her support for their ideas and abilities."

"THANKS, YOU DID A GREAT JOB!"

With those words, the Georgia Appalachian Trail Club acknowledged the contributions of Margaret Drummond toward leading, promoting, and growing the club. The statement is very simple and direct, mimicking Margaret's earlier insistence to, "Just call me Margaret."

Margaret continued to serve on ATC's board of managers as a chair emeritus until 2005, completing twenty-six years of volunteer service to the organization when the bylaws for the renamed organization did not allow for the emeritus positions.

For those within ATC and her Georgia club who for decades thought of her as a special friend, there was a growing sadness as Margaret gradually withdrew from many of her Trail activities. Those friends closest to her, such as Marianne Skeen, Rosalind Van Landingham, George Owen, and Dave Sherman, coped in various ways with an often saddening sense of separation from Margaret. Over time, they began to understand that Margaret's withdrawal was not reflective of any change in their friendship, but rather due to her difficulty in accepting her increasing inability to participate in the Trail activities she so long enjoyed. Marianne recalled, in particular, that once Margaret found it necessary to use a walker to get about, she withdrew even more and would agree to only occasionally go out to lunch with Marianne.

In interviews, Dave, in particular, looked back with sorrow to those occasions when Margaret would no longer respond to his overtures of friendship: letters unanswered, telephone calls never returned. Her friends within the Trail community felt her absence, and they missed the good times they once shared. We can only speculate that Margaret was experiencing the same sense of loss, and withdrawing was the only response she could offer.

Margaret's death in April 2015 was met with sadness by many within the GATC and ATC. In leadership positions as president of the Georgia club and chair of ATC, Margaret consistently demonstrated a mastery of promoting partnerships, inclusiveness, and committee work. Margaret Drummond's journey from Trail walker to Trail maintainer and finally to Trail preservationist bears witness to her love of the Trail and her commitment to its governance. The hallmark of her service to GATC and ATC was to validate the then-Conference and its maintaining clubs' roles as guardians of the Appalachian Trail.

For Margaret, preservation of this special, natural place became a life's work. Margaret — "accidentally born" in Oklahoma and appropriately laid to rest in her beloved Atlanta, Georgia — worked to preserve the southern-most section of the Appalachian Trail and grew to treasure its entire length.

Hikers near Katahdin in 1932.

Taking a break in Nahmakanta Lake after the 1939 conference. ATC
Secretary Marion Park at right.

NOT THE LAST WORDS:

WHY THESE WOMEN?

Jean Stephenson's life centered on the Appalachian Trail, and in particular, she loved the Maine woods. She stood up, fought down, and in every way pushed on with the Trail project, beginning in its formative years. She insisted that the Appalachian Trail Conference needed a newsletter, so she paid for the printing of the first issues and she stayed at the helm as editor for more than twenty-five years. She faced off with the lumbering companies in Maine whose industry threatened the solitude of the North Woods. Where Myron Avery was focused on completing the Trail, Jean centered her efforts on ensuring its perpetuity.

Ruth Blackburn also feared what could be lost. She went into action whenever she perceived that land acquisitions were moving too slowly, particularly in the central Appalachians. She schooled herself on property ownership, pestered state and federal officials on the urgency to purchase lands that were critical to creating a continuous trail corridor, and stoically presented requests to federal appropriations subcommittees for funds to continue land acquisitions. Although mostly known for her quiet disposition, she saw demons in the future and was determined to ward them off.

Margaret Drummond insisted upon professionalism among the volunteer maintainers. She worked to establish a healthy balance among the independent thinking trail workers, the oversight staff of the ATC, and the institutionalism of the National Park Service. Of the three women, she alone spoke about an awareness that certain environments were inhibiting to women.

Simply stated, these women were chosen for this history because they committed themselves to what Benton MacKaye called "the magnificent fight." And to each effort, they brought sets of skills particularly their own, magnified by their passion for the Appalachian Trail project.

Also contributing to the selection of these three women is the fact that their contributions occurred at particular turning points in Appalachian Trail history. Their influences were felt during particular chapters in Trail history, and perhaps their contributions actually helped to define the chapters. During the early years of trail building, Jean was instrumental in laying a strong organizational foundation. Ruth's influence was felt during the middle years when securing the corridor was of prime importance. Margaret's influence was felt as the conference morphed into the modern-day conservancy and the role of volunteers was reaffirmed.

Lastly, Jean Stephenson, Ruth Blackburn, and Margaret Drummond were chosen for the inspiration and relevance their stories have for today's Appalachian Trail women. To the credit of all the early A.T. clubs, women have long contributed to the Trail project — occasionally limited by the social mores of the times in which they lived — but nonetheless recognized, affirmed, and welcomed by their male Trail peers.

Not all have been volunteers. Pamela Underhill — whose father had played key roles for the Interior Department Bureau of Outdoor Recreation in developing the 1968 National Trails System Act — was the longest serving super-

intendent of the Appalachian National Scenic Trail in the National Park Service, from 1995 to 2013. As she is described in the Appalachian Trail Museum's Hall of Fame, "Throughout her career [from 1973 on], but especially in her capacity as park manager, Ms. Underhill has displayed an unswerving devotion to the A.T., to ATC, to volunteer-based stewardship, and to the A.T. cooperative management system. She has been a strong and articulate advocate for land conservation along the A.T., even at some risk to her own professional career. She was equally forceful in defending and supporting the unique partnership that exists among ATPO, ATC, the trail-maintaining clubs, and Appalachian Trail volunteers — within her own agency, with other federal and state agencies, and with the public at large."

Now in the twenty-first century, women continue to participate at every level of the A.T. project. Their trail work in every way and every day affirms the statement, proclaims the truth, "We were there, too." To celebrate the many modern-day female Trail workers, I invited a few to reflect upon their Trail work. Here is what they had to say.

DIANNA CHRISTOPULOS

I like to play outside, and, quite frankly, the Appalachian Trail seduced me one brilliant October day in 2000 when the fall color change was at its peak. I knew about the Trail and had even hiked parts of it, but it held no magic for me until I climbed south out of Harpers Ferry, West Virginia, to see the surrounding landscapes spread out before me in orange, red, and yellow cloaks. My view was cast all the way to tiny airplanes taking off and landing at Dulles Airport forty miles away in northern Virginia. Standing there, being passed by hikers headed in both directions, I could FEEL that I was connected to Maine and Georgia and could go there if I just kept walking.

In 2008, I completed the A.T. after nine years of section-hiking. In the meantime, my husband and I had moved from Dallas, Texas, to Roanoke, Virginia, for retirement and joined the Roanoke Appalachian Trail Club. I would have been happy filling my retirement years with hiking and leading hikes, but things happened.

In late 2014, a Pittsburgh fracking company announced that it wanted to build a 300-mile natural-gas pipeline right through our part of the world. At first, I did not think much about it. So what? There are pipelines everywhere. I was soon to learn otherwise, as I studied more about this industry and its impact on the natural environment. My attentions became more and more focused upon Mountain Valley Pipeline (MVP) and a plague of similar pipeline projects springing up all along the East Coast. I soon discovered:

- They are huge, dangerous, and intended for overseas and out-of-state use.
- They follow extremely destructive routes that are steep, forested slopes in the mountains and sinkhole-filled karst in the valleys.
- In the case of Mountain Valley Pipeline, the project would leave a huge scar visible for 80 to 100 miles from locations such as Angel's Rest, Rice Field, Symms Gap, and Kelly Knob — a fact that quickly engaged the Appalachian Trail Conservancy in opposition to the project.
- In addition, MVP is a massive threat to water quality, endangered species, and public safety in every county it would touch. Trained local volunteers have documented hundreds of water violations since the project started construction, resulting in a lawsuit against MVP from Virginia's attorney general.

- And, the gas produced is not even intended for local use. Almost all gas will be shipped out of state or overseas. Why? Because a Pittsburgh fracking company has a surplus of product and can use the federal- and state-granted power of eminent domain to take private property while making a fifteen percent net profit for operating the pipeline.

This very questionable project has unified landowners, conservation, and recreation groups and local governments, regardless of their political leanings. It has produced tree-sitters, lawsuits, rallies, thousands of detailed filings to federal and state agencies, and a stop-work order across the Appalachian Trail and in Jefferson National Forest. The project as of mid-2020 was already two years behind schedule and about fifty percent over budget. Wall Street analysts were beginning to question MVP's viability, threatening sources of borrowed money, its lifeblood.

My own participation has been rather nerdy. I read technical documents, write formal comments, give lectures and speeches, send letters and commentaries to newspaper editors, visit people who can help us, share with journalists, find consultants, and simply do my best to fill in the gaps and give encouragement, while landowners, students, lawyers, and staff members from groups like the Sierra Club, Appalachian Mountain Advocates, and the Southern Environmental Law Center go after the company for its continuing shady behavior. I share their motto: WANGA — "We are not going away." This land is our land.

ATC in August 2020 signed an agreement under which MVP agreed to pay $19.2 million for damages to the A.T. experience and to local tourism-based economies. The Conservancy retained full freedom to contest permits still lacking from multiple agencies. WANGA.

Diana Christopulos

Dr. Christopulos had careers as a college professor, nonprofit executive, and owner of an international management consulting business before she retired in 2003. Past president of the Roanoke A.T. Club, she is currently a member of the Appalachian Trail Conservancy's President's Leadership Council and immediate past president of the Blue Ridge Land Conservancy, as well as an adjunct assistant professor of biology at Hollins University. She was the winner of the 2019 national Cox Conserves Hero award. She and her partner, Mark McClain, live in Salem, Virginia.

KAREN LUTZ

My career with the Appalachian Trail Conference began in 1988 when I was thrilled to be hired by Bob Proudman to serve as the Conference's mid-Atlantic regional representative. Ten years earlier, in 1978, I had completed a thru-hike of the Appalachian Trail while taking a break from graduate school at Penn State, where I was pursuing a master's degree in outdoor recreation. While a number of great women were on ATC's staff at the time I was hired, I was the second to be brought on board in a "field" position.

My female colleagues within the Conference served in more traditional clerical positions or, like the beloved Jean Cashin, in information-services roles. My male counterparts, serving as regional representatives elsewhere, were all a foot taller than me but welcomed me with their equally impressive big hearts. As I began my work with the Conference, my role was different, but, from the beginning, I was not treated differently. I was part of the Trail team.

Early in my career, I understood that building relationships with partners, including volunteer trail clubs and agencies, would be critical to my success, as well as the success of ATC and its mission. I very soon discovered that the trail clubs were, for the most part, dominated by older men, born and raised in a generation and culture somewhat different than the (sometimes) seemingly more liberal 20th century.

I worked hard and developed a reasonably good skill set. And, most likely, the fact that I had completed a hike of the entire Trail opened an otherwise closed door for me. I made many friends, shared many experiences, and grew professionally in many ways. My thirty-year stint at ATC gave me an opportunity to cross paths with some extraordinary people. And a couple total pains in the butt. Yes, my many years in the "field" revealed that Trail people are independent, diverse, and, in some cases, beyond my understanding. But, they all shared a love for that "long, brown path."

I also worked closely with dozens of government-agency staff members — from small municipalities to large federal agencies — and built some life-long friendships and wonderful professional relationships with those civil servants. Looking back over the years, I have come to realize that I enjoyed most working with dedicated, talented, hard-working, committed volunteers who truly represent the soul of the Trail.

In 1988, when I began working for ATC, the National Park Service's land-acquisition efforts were in high gear, identifying, negotiating, and acquiring properties to ensure a continuous, protected corridor. I was intimately aware of these efforts. Since 1978, as a volunteer and founding member of what became the Cumberland Valley Appalachian Trail Club, much of my effort went into coordinating with club leadership and the National Park Service to design an optimal corridor within Pennsylvania's Cumberland Valley. The goal was to best protect and provide a high-quality A.T. experience. Many public meetings, a few handfuls of disgruntled landowners, and an exceptionally patient and gifted team of Park Service realty specialists resulted in the Trail experience hikers enjoy today through the Cumberland Valley.

As both a Trail-club volunteer and an ATC staff member, I consider the acquisition work in the Cumberland Valley as a highlight of my Trail career.

As director of the mid-Atlantic region, I was fortunate to be able to have a leadership role with agency partners on what some might consider legacy trail projects. At the very least, they are construction projects that will be there for a very long time. Together, we worked to improve road-crossing safety by building a pedestrian bridge that spans a hairpin blind turn on Pa. 225 in Dauphin County and building the first-of-its-kind pedestrian underpass under the busy Pa. 944 in Cumberland County. Working with volunteers and the New Jersey Department of Environmental Protection, we designed and constructed a mile-long, helical-pier-supported, elevated boardwalk to span an exceptional wetland and provide hikers with an extraordinary hiking experience in Vernon. Years later, a similar, albeit somewhat shorter, boardwalk was designed and built in Pawling, New York.

The saddest experience of my career was my involvement with the investigation, trial, and conviction of the brutal murderer of southbound thru-hikers Molly LaRue and Geoff Hood. While out with a long-time volunteer and a colleague doing trail design in Cumberland County, we observed the killer just days before the victims' bodies were found. During the trial, I served as the prosecution's lead witness and testified on a number of facts. Part of my testimony was intended to explain the A.T., the thru-hiking culture, and the extraordinary community that is involved with its management.

Long after the suspect was convicted, state police leaders told me that the facts of the case — two transient victims and a transient assailant in a very remote location — should have been a nearly impossible case to solve. However, because of the help provided to them by members of the A.T. community, it was the easiest homicide case they ever worked. Years later, as I look back on this sad experience, I'm very proud to have been a member of the Trail community that shared the many emotions surrounding this tragedy and banded together for justice and healing.

Through all my Trail experiences, spanning many decades and many positions, I have come to realize that my contributions are part of a long history of Trail work and Trail workers. During the years of service given by Jean Stephenson, Ruth Blackburn, Margaret Drummond, and today's Appalachian Trail women such as myself, the Trail has been a great equalizer.

Formal education, wealth, gender, age, profession, and other "worldly" characteristics take a back stage to the spirit that knits together all those who work to protect the Appalachian Trail. My career was blessed with this spirit that continues to grow and embrace the next generation of Trail workers.

Karen Lutz

Karen Lutz retired from the Appalachian Trail Conservancy in late 2018 and is still enjoying the outdoors and still involved in local Appalachian Trail issues.

SANDRA MARRA

On or about 1987, I found myself involved with the Potomac Appalachian Trail Club (PATC), somehow making my way onto the council as the general secretary — with little knowledge and even less experience. But, the Appalachian Trail had caught both my attention and my imagination, and I wanted to not just volunteer and manage the Trail but also I wanted to learn to hike it.

Growing up in urban New Jersey, my family did not spend a lot of time out in the woods. Vacations were trips "back home" to Pennsylvania or "down to the shore." My first experiences with hiking were the PATC day hikes in and out of work sites. (The first project I worked on was the construction of Rod Hollow Shelter.) But, I wanted most was to experience backpacking. As you can imagine, I suffered no shortage of gear advice, as well as thoughts on where and when I should have my first experiences.

My first backpack was an external-frame (red!) backpack. When you added in a sleeping bag and Thermarest, packable pillow (!), food, stove, water bottles, too many changes of clothes, and heavy camp shoes, I was probably hovering around plus-forty-five pounds. But, I was also in my twenties, so what I lacked in sense I made up for in youth and energy.

I found I really loved the experience. I loved that everything I needed to take care of myself I could pack in this bag on my back. I loved that I could see things and go places that could only be accessed by helicopter or my own two feet. And, I loved the community I found on not just the A.T. but all the trails I hiked.

In the 1980s, there were not a lot of women in that community. I had a group from PATC that hiked together. Trail clubs have a long and rich history of women members working side-by-side with the men, making equal contributions, but, in general, we girls were in the minority.

My experience in leadership roles often mirrored what I found out on the Trail. Although there were certainly women in club leadership and on ATC's board, our numbers usually could be counted on one hand. With PATC, I moved from general secretary to vice president and eventually became the third woman president in 1996. In 1999, I joined the ATC board and was there when we made the important decision to change our name and our public focus from Conference to Conservancy. I was a member of the first stewardship council of the Conservancy and then moved back to board roles, eventually as a member of the board in 2008. In 2013, I became chair of the Conservancy — a role that had been held previously by only two other women, both profiled here.

And then suddenly, in the summer of 2019, I was asked to step into the role of chief executive officer. My travels through the leadership ranks is somewhat reflective of a changing environment for women and the A.T. We are there in greater numbers across all wilderness recreation activities, as I see in my role as a member of the Partnership for the National Trails System board. We come in all shapes and sizes, ages and colors; we come together with male and female partners; or we tackle the experiences on our own. But, while much has changed, there is still a long way to go. Women and people of color are still in the minority on our trails. Staffs of conservation nonprofits (ATC included) continue to be predominantly white and often predominately male (ATC excluded). Boards fare even worse, where older, white men still represent the majority of nonprofit leadership.

This is still a journey for all of us. Ensuring inclusivity is not a passive endeavor. We need to invite, encourage, and mentor everyone with the interest and desire to experience the out-of-doors as a whole and most especially our very special trail.

Sandi Marra

Sandi Marra is president & CEO of the Appalachian Trail Conservancy in Harpers Ferry and married to Chris Brunton, a leading PATC Trail maintainer.

PAT YALE

The advertisement read, "Help build a piece of the Appalachian Trail." When my daughter said, "Mom, we should do this!" I agreed and signed us both up. What began as a week of learning to build stone retaining walls has now turned into twenty-six years, and counting, of working to maintain and improve the Trail we all cherish.

My involvement in the support of the Trail has provided an endless variety of opportunities, from the physical labor of trail maintenance to administrative support for special projects. I have served in many capacities, including president of a trail-maintaining club and member, then chair, of the Pennsylvania Appalachian Trail Committee. I have enjoyed several seasonal and part-time employment positions with the Appalachian Trail Conservancy, and I was part of two small paid crews doing temporary trail relocations.

As a boundary technician, I recovered a surveyed boundary that no one had seen for twenty years. I've used surveyor-grade GPS units to take coordinates to help complete the GIS mapping of Appalachian Trail lands. My trail leadership roles include serving several times as camp coordinator for the Mid-Atlantic Trail Crew, an experience that involved planning meals and purchasing food to feed these hard-working folks. And, lastly, I am particularly proud of my service as a boundary monitor and comaintainer for the Susquehanna Appalachian Trail Club, where my certification by the Forest Service to operate a chainsaw allows me to cut blowdowns — trees that have fallen across the footpath, typically as the result of a storm.

In 2015 and 2016, I assisted the mid-Atlantic regional clubs and office staff with the asset-inventory project. This was a huge effort to place a dollar value on the "assets" or structures of the Trail. Work involved counting rock steps and water bars; measuring shelters, privies, bridges, and parking lots; and GPS mapping of side trails. Everyone, volunteers and staff alike, put a tremendous effort into this project in order to position the A.T. within our national park system on an equal status with the other well-known national parks, thereby ensuring that the Trail receives the visibility (and funding!) from Washington it deserves.

I consider myself as following in the footsteps of women such as Jean Stephenson, Ruth Blackburn, and Margaret Drummond because I have passionately enjoyed my A.T. work. And, the work I've enjoyed the most is my physical labor, offered during nearly one hundred weeks of Trail crew!

I've helped build shelters and tear down timber-framed barns, dig ditches and set stepping stones, build turnpike and rock steps, build puncheon through wet areas, build boardwalks through really wet areas, and make "crush and fill" by using a sledge hammer to break big rocks into small rocks. Countless hours spent doing those types of hard, physical labor are always my good times.

One of my favorite crew projects was the relocation and rebuild of the A.T. on Bear Mountain in New York. As a member of the Mid-Atlantic Crew, I worked on the mountain every year of this remarkable thirteen-year project. Each year, crew members worked as a team on Bear Mountain to give back to the Trail all that it has come to mean in our lives. Perhaps due to the complexity of this project and the many demands it put on my physical abilities, I am exceedingly proud to have been a part of this important part of the history of the Appalachian Trail.

Like the women in this book, I have had the opportunity to support the Appalachian Trail in a variety of ways — getting down and dirty in the hands-on jobs of Trail crew and maintenance, attending and participating in meetings to shape the future of the trail, and sometimes simply sitting at a computer inputting data. Having completed a section-hike of the Trail in 2015, I also treasure my time spent just putting my boots on the trail to hike my favorite sections and experience its natural beauty.

Through all of my Trail experiences, I have come to realize why it is so important for us to maintain this "footpath for those who seek fellowship with the wilderness." The A.T. is maintained by a large group of very dedicated volunteers, and I am proud to help continue the legacy of this beautiful and majestic trail.

Pat Yale

After retiring from the business world, Pat and her husband, Neal Watson, moved to a cabin in the forest just a half-mile from the Appalachian Trail. They live a simple lifestyle and enjoy camping and traveling. Since 2002, they have hiked more than 13,500 miles, mostly in the United States. Supporting the A.T. is a family affair; both of Pat's daughters have volunteered on ATC Trail crews.

Bibliography

Books

Anderson, Larry. *Benton MacKaye: Conservationist, Planner, and Creator of the Appalachian Trail.* Baltimore, Maryland: The Johns Hopkins University Press, 2002.

Bates, David. *Breaking Trail in the Central Appalachians — a Narrative.* Washington, D.C.: *The Potomac Appalachian* Trail Club, 1987.

Boardman, Julie. *When Women and Mountains Meet: Adventures in the White Mountains.* Etna, New Hampshire: The Durand Press, 2001.

Brown, Rebecca A. *Women on High: Pioneers of Mountaineering.* Boston, Massachusetts: The Appalachian Mountain Club, 2002.

Georgia Appalachian Trail Club History Committee. *Friendships of the Trail: The History of the Georgia Appalachian Trail Club, 1930-1980.* Atlanta, Georgia: Georgia Appalachian Trail Club, Inc., 1995.

Georgia Appalachian Trail Club History Subcommittee. *Friendships of the Trail: 1981-1990, A Chronology of Activities Both On and Off the Trail.* Atlanta, Georgia: Georgia Appalachian Trail Club, Inc., 2004.

King, Brian B. *The Appalachian Trail: Celebrating America's Hiking Trail.* New York, N.Y.: Appalachian Trail Conservancy and Rizzoli International Publications, Inc., 2012.

Niedzaliek, Carol. *A Footpath in the Wilderness: The Early Days of PATC.* Vienna, Virginia: Potomac Appalachian Trail Club, 2003.

Waterman, Laura and Guy. *Forest and Crag, A History of Hiking, Trail Blazing, and Adventure in the Northeast Mountains.* Boston, Massachusetts: Appalachian Mountain Club, 1989.

Welts Kaufman, Polly. *National Parks and the Women's Voice: A History.* Albuquerque, New Mexico: University of New Mexico Press, 2006.

PERIODICALS

Appalachian Trailway News, 1939 to 1964.
Appalachian Trailway News, March/April 1979.
Appalachian Trailway News, Golden Anniversary Issue, January 1989.
Appalachian Trailway News, July/August 2000.
Potomac Appalachian Trail Club Bulletin, October 1934, April 1935, July 1935, January 1936, October 1936, January 1937, April 1938, October 1938, January 1939, April 1939, July 1941.

ARTICLES

Appalachian Trail Conference. "Ruth E. Blackburn." *Appalachian Trailway News,* March/April 2004, pp. 13-15.

Bennett, Anne. "Jean Stephenson." *Appalachian Trailway News,* January 1989, pp. 16-19.

Emory University. "Profile." *Campus Report,* October 30, 1978.

Georgia Appalachian Trail Club, "Margaret Chairs ATC." *The Georgia Mountaineer,* August 1989, pp. 1, 3.

— "Friend of the Trail Honorees." *The Georgia Mountaineer,* February 1993, pp. 1, 3.

— "GATC Member Margaret Drummond Receives Honorary ATC Membership." *The Georgia Mountaineer,* October 1997, p. 1.

— "Spotlight on Margaret Drummond." *The Georgia Mountaineer,* November 2005, pp. 1-2.

Jenner, Judy. "Just call me Margaret." *Appalachian Trailway News,* September/October 1995, pp. 11-13.

— "Fred and Ruth Blackburn: First Couple of the Appalachian Trail." *Appalachian Trailway News,* November/December 1984, pp. 16-20.

Nichol, Florence. "In Memoriam: Jean Stephenson, 1983-1979." *Appalachian Trailway News,* March/April 1979, p. 14.

Niedzaliek, Carol. "A Tribute to Ruth E. Blackburn." *The Potomac Appalachian,* March 2004, p. 7.

Potomac Appalachian Trail Club. "Blackburn Trail Center Renovations Planned." *The Potomac Appalachian,* February 1997, pp 1, 5.

— "Honorary Life Member, Jean Stephenson." *The Potomac Appalachian,* March 1978, p. 3.

— "Jean Stephenson Room." *The Potomac Appalachian*, May 1979, p. 8.

Stephenson, Jean. "Impressions of the Maine Wilderness." *In the Maine Woods*, July 1941.

— "The Appalachian Trail–What is it?" January 1948.

— "The Appalachian Trail." *The Phi Delta Delta*, May 1936.

— "Camping at Katahdin." *Appalachia*, June 1955, pp. 339-340.

— "Appalachian Scenic Footpath." *The Commonwealth*, November 1938.

Strain, Paula. "The Blackburns: PATC's Foreign Ministers." *The Potomac Appalachian*, November 2000, pp. 4, 6.

— "The Blackburns: PATC's Foreign Ministers, Part II." *The Potomac Appalachian*, December 2000, pp. 6, 13.

— "The Blackburns: PATC's Foreign Ministers, Part III." *The Potomac Appalachian*, January 2001, pp. 9-10.

Walker, Dorothy. "Kindred Spirits." *Potomac Appalachian Trail Club Bulletin*, November 1977, pp. 10-18.

CORRESPONDENCE

Stephenson, Jean:

From David Field to Brian King, November 26, 1995, Jean Stephenson biography.

From Jean Stephenson to various people, September 20, 1938, to May 3, 1973, Maine Appalachian Trail Club Archives.

From Jean Stephenson to Sam Butcher *et al.*, April 30, 1973, Maine Appalachian Trail Club Archives.

Blackburn, Ruth:

From Ruth Blackburn to U.S. House of Representatives Interior and Insular Affairs Appropriations Subcommittee, March 6, 1979. PATC Archives. Folder 1980-1.

From Ruth Blackburn to U.S. House of Representatives Interior and Insular Affairs Appropriations Subcommittee, March 17, 1980. PATC Archives. Folder 1980-1.

From Ruth Blackburn to U.S. House of Representatives Interior and Insular Affairs Appropriations Subcommittee, February 24, 1981. PATC Archives. Folder 1980-1.

From Charles W. Sloan to Laurence R. Van Meter, April 19, 1982. PATC Archives. Folder Chuck Sloan. Legal.

INTERVIEWS

Douglas, Darcy, by telephone, January 8, 2018.
Drummond, Margaret, by telephone, October 15, 2009.
Field, David, by telephone, November 7, 2008.
Jenner, Judy, by telephone, November 6, 2008.
King, Brian, Harpers Ferry, West Virginia, February 13, 2009.
Skeen, Marianne, by telephone, October 30, 2009.
Startzell, David, Harpers Ferry, West Virginia, September 30, 2009, and April 1, 2011.
Van Landingham, Rosalind, by telephone, November 20, 2009.

ARCHIVES

Appalachian Trail Conservancy Archives

James, Harlean: Scrapbook No. 1, 1927-1929; No. 7, 1938-1939.
Stephenson, Jean: Scrapbook No. 6, 1936-37.
> Box F-1-3, 1930-1939, *Appalachian Trailway News*, Vol. 1, January 1939 to Vol. 7, No. 2, May 1946.
> Box 2-1-5, *Appalachian Trailway News*, March/April 1979, "In Memoriam, Jean Stephenson, 1893-1979."
> Box 3-2-5, Stephenson Correspondence 1934-1938; Stephenson Correspondence 1938-1942; Stephenson Correspondence 1942; Stephenson Correspondence 1944.
> Box 3-2-6, Stephenson Trail Reports 1949; Stephenson Correspondence 1951; Stephenson Girl Scout Project Planning and Preparation 1955; Stephenson Correspondence 1952-1961; Stephenson Correspondence Re: Trail Manual (ATC, No. 1), 1965; Stephenson ATN Correspondence 1960-1972.

Blackburn, Ruth:
> Box 1-2-2. A.T. Conference Employee Personnel Policy, Transition Correspondence: Personnel/Staff.
> Box 1-2-3. 1983-A.T. Patches, bumper stickers.
> Box 5-4-3. ATC 1975-1977. Selection Committee.

Drummond, Margaret:
> Box 3-1-2. *Appalachian Trailway News*, January 1989, September/October 1989, November/December 1989, March/April 1990, July/

August 1990, March/April 1992, May/June 1992, July/August 1992, September/October 1992, November/December 1992.
Box 3-1-3. *Appalachian Trailway News*, 1992-1994.

Potomac Appalachian Club Archives
Stephenson, Jean:
    Box 3. Committee Publicity; Cabins-Shelters News; Correspondence Miscellany.
    Box 4. Reminiscences; Schairer, Frank, Jr.–Supervisor of Trails; Shelters; Supervisor of Trails–Materials 1930s; Pennsylvania Forest Service.
    Box 6. Excursions Committee 1940-1946.
Blackburn, Ruth:
    Box 3 (1927-1939), Excursions Committee and Excursions: Maine Trips 1939 ATC.
    Box 4, MacKaye, Benton
    Box 8, Map Making Book 1950-54, and G.F. Blackburn–President PATC 1953-55.
    Fred Blackburn Diary
    Box 11, Blackburn, Ruth: President 1965-67; Committee: Trail Lands Study 1971-74; The Blackburns: PATC's Foreign Ministers.
    Box 17 (1970-1977), Committee – Government Relations, 1976-77, Committee – Government Relations: West Virginia, 1972-1976.

POETRY

"The Catoctin Hills," by Jean Stephenson. PATC Archives, Box 4, "Poems."

WEB SITES

American Society of Genealogists

SOURCES OF PHOTOGRAPHS

Appalachian Trail Conservancy Archives — pages 11, 14 lower, 15, 23–26, 49 top, 50 except left, 51–52, 53 except middle, 72, 87 top right and lower, 88, 89 top and lower left, 90 all except middle right, 91 top and lower right, 105–106, 132 except top right, 133 except top right, 134, 135, 158, and 165. Middle photograph on page 103 was taken by M. Gentry.

Appalachian Trail Museum Society — page 160.

Dartmouth College Library Special Collections — page 8.

Georgia Appalachian Trail Club — 131, 132 top right, and 133 top right.

Library of Congress — pages 12 and 14 upper.

Potomac Appalachian Trail Club Archives — pages 49, 50 left, 53 middle, 87 top and middle left, 89 lower right, 90 middle right, and 91 lower left.

Shirley Historical Society — page 9.

Unusualhistoricals.blogspot.com — page 2.

Carol Avery Vimtrup Family Album, courtesy of David B. Field — page 19.

Provided by subject — pages 161, 163, 167.